BEYOND REVOLUTION
A Response to the Underground Church

BOOKS BY THOMAS C. ODEN
Published by The Westminster Press

Beyond Revolution:
A Response to the Underground Church
Contemporary Theology and Psychotherapy
Kerygma and Counseling
Radical Obedience: The Ethics of Rudolf Bultmann

BEYOND REVOLUTION

A Response to the Underground Church

by
THOMAS C. ODEN

THE WESTMINSTER PRESS
Philadelphia

ISBN 0–664–24895–0

Library of Congress Catalog Card No. 72–120409

PUBLISHED BY THE WESTMINSTER PRESS®
PHILADELPHIA, PENNSYLVANIA

PRINTED IN THE UNITED STATES OF AMERICA

For my brother, Tal—
astute critic
gifted innovator
persuasive partner in dialogue
trustworthy companion
with gratitude and affection

Contents

Preface

The dilemma for many today is not the classical question of whether salvation is possible apart from the church, but on the contrary, whether it is possible within the church. A growing number of sensitive innovators in the renewing church have come sincerely to feel that the institutional church is so utterly captive to inauthenticity that the only moral alternative is not only to work outside it but to work against it. Some of our sharpest young theological minds are saying, with Michael Novak, "The prospects for reform in the institutional Church leave many of us bored."[1]

Surely there are times when every serious churchman is appalled at the insensitivity and callousness of the institutional church. Anyone who fails to see these shortcomings of the church is taking the church with less seriousness than it would wish to have itself taken.

Anyone who has examined the growing corpus of recent literature on "Why I Quit the Ministry" and "Why I Am Leaving the Church"[2] should be aware by now that there are some very good reasons for leaving the church. What is really required in our time is that someone show why believing, loving, and concerned persons should stay *in* the church.

I am aware of the fact that this argument might have

been quite different in a different historical context. It has unfolded as a direct response to a specific situation: the crisis in institutional continuity in both church and society. The risk that any commentator must take in speaking to a rapidly changing situation is that by the time his message is delivered the situation may have changed significantly enough to alter its relevance. But amid the crisis which is our times, that is a risk we must be willing to embrace with joy.

The crisis to which I am responding is the sudden burgeoning of a necro-ecclesiology which argues not only that the church is dead and that faith must learn to live without the church, but, more so, that what remains of the church must will its own death, in order to live anew incognito in the modern world. It is not surprising that in a deteriorating cultural setting the theme of death should become a pervasive theme of theological reflection. Likewise it is not accidental that the "death of God" movement has been followed by a "death of the church" movement. For a necro-theology can be succeeded only by a necro-ecclesiology. What is a bit surprising is that the full resources of responsible theological reflection have not been applied to the issues raised in these developments.

Portions of Chapters 1, 2, and 10 have appeared in *The Christian Century, motive,* and *Christian Advocate,* and portions of Chapters 1 and 9 may be seen in an embryonic form in my previous discussion of *The Community of Celebration* (Nashville: The National Methodist Student Movement, 1964), which was noncommercially distributed through local branches of the student Christian movement but was never available to the general public.

To Albert C. Outler and James M. Gustafson I am profoundly indebted for much of the substructure of this exploration, though I do not wish them to be held responsible for any inadequacies discovered in the argument. Illuminating discussions by Hans Küng, Gregory Baum, Peter Berger, James Dittes, Wolfhart Pannenberg, and Harvey Cox have been my constant and respected partners in dialogue. Among writers with whom I have substantially disagreed, but found their work immensely valuable for my reflection, are Charles Davis, Stephen Rosc, Malcolm Boyd, William Hamilton, and Herbert Marcuse. Among my colleagues and friends with whom I have struggled often with these issues, I wish especially to express my gratitude to Frank Mabee, William B. Oden, Stephen Wells, William A. Holmes, and above all my brother, Tal, to whom this book is affectionately dedicated. For help with the manuscript, I am grateful to Roger Hall, Jonna Hansmeier, James York, and Linda Ammons. Finally, not only for personal support and understanding but also for critical help in articulating this argument, I am deeply grateful to my wife, Edrita.

T. C. O.

Part I

THE CRISIS IN CONTINUITY

Chapter 1

On Ecclesial Patricide

It is not merely that the church is like an old friend whom we see now failing in health. It is more as if we suspected that someone were plotting to "do in" this ailing old friend.

Some people experience the current situation as a curious question of ecclesiastical euthanasia. The analogy is drawn like this: It is as if the current institutional structures of the church were in a death coma. There is no hope for the patient. The blood is still flowing, but there is too much damaged tissue to hope for recovery. Technology and abundance allow us to keep the patient alive in a lung machine, but only with frequent blood transfusions and intensive care.

The moral question becomes: Should we let the organism die? What if others desperately need the lung machine? What if suffering is so intense that the act of allowing the patient to die would be an act of mercy? In short, would it be better to go ahead and pull the church's plug? Some think this is the appropriate analogy for the current situation; some argue that the plug should be pulled immediately. Why? Because in a world of accelerating hunger and poverty, it is too expensive to keep a dying, hopeless, vegetating organism alive by purely artificial means. If the plug were pulled, the extravagant resources and intensive care that it takes to keep the organism alive could be redirected toward more needy, more hopeful, more promising causes.

The analogy, of course, depends upon the assumption that the church is in fact in its last coma.[1] Although we have no doubt that certain institutional forms of the church are dying, this does not mean that the church itself, the living tradition of the apostles, prophets, and martyrs, is thereby phasing out, since the church is greater than any one of its institutional manifestations.

It can be argued that there may be special circumstances when the best thing for a cell or a limb or an organism is to let it die, especially if the pain is intense and unbearable, with no hope whatever for recovery. Although this may be the condition of some senile institutional structures, it is hardly the condition of the Christian tradition as a whole in the modern world. Admittedly, it is sometimes very difficult to bump off an institution, since institutions often find ways of perpetuating their progeny beyond all usefulness. That may be true of some stubborn institutional church forms, but it can hardly be applied to all of them. There may be times when we will have to plot to "do in" certain dysfunctional parts of the organism, but surely that does not imply the uniform uselessness of all church institutions.

Is tyrannicide a more appropriate image? Is killing the church today more like killing an unjust, powerful tyrant whose most demonic quality is precisely his capacity to maintain his power? Some branches of the ecclesial organism doubtless deserve to be viewed as tyrannical, and the rights of men to commit tyrannicide on behalf of the future of the whole organism are certainly debatable, but again the analogy is far too limited to be applied generally to the church as a whole.

What do we do with the church now that we have entered the threshold of the postmodern world? Do we just allow it to live out its last days in peace? Do we murder the old girl? Do we pull the plug? Do we plot for a quick assassination?[2]

All these images depend upon one faulty assumption: that the historic church itself is to be finally identified, unequivocally and unambiguously with certain familiar, distorted forms. We are struggling to see the church in a larger historical perspective than our particular limited circumstances. We are trying to perceive both its mutations and its continuities in many different historical settings, so as to deprive us of the illusion that any one institutional manifestation comprises the wholeness of the church.

Most churchmen with one eye and half a nostril can see and smell the stench in the church. Who needs hackneyed criticisms? It is evident that the condition of Christian institutions today is defensive, confused, and in many respects uncreative, but this is also the condition of all the institutions of Western society. In fact, every social institution over twenty years of age has had its credibility challenged.

I would like to propose a mild counterthesis to the subterraneans who argue that the institutional church *ipso facto* is irrecoverable and that alternatives must be sought outside these defensive structures. My thesis: Despite all the talk of "action now," the underground strategy often becomes a subtle rationale for inaction. It is an easy means of dismissing the tougher problems of corporate reconstruction, a dodge of the harder assignment of creating authentic Christian community in our time. The ecclesial muckrakers see clearly that the church must undergo fundamental transformation. They sense that the task is monumental. We all would wish to be exempted from such an enormous task. One way to relieve oneself of guilt, at least temporarily, is by self-righteously debunking the parent structures. Those who seem to call for a movement underground may be moving away from, rather than toward, the character of radical responsibility to which they so easily appeal.

There can be no reform of the church without the church. The renewal of the church cannot simply be synonymous with its death. Although the death of certain cancerous forms may make possible the development of more healthy forms, that does not imply that the reform of the organism as a whole simply depends upon whether and how fast it can die. That is a cynical, suicidal oversimplification.

It is a political axiom that to withdraw from involvement in structures of power is unconsciously to affirm the *status quo*.[3] Such is the undesired result of much despair of sincere churchmen over the inadequacies of the church, if it prompts them to lapse from serious involvement in institutional reconstruction. The surest way to rubber-stamp the *status quo* in the institutional church today is to withdraw from creative involvement in it.

Can responsible churchmen turn their backs upon a tubercular institutional church? A general viewpoint has prevailed among many perceptive, committed persons within the renewing church, which runs something like this: The present institutional structures are so backward, so introverted, so hard to work with, so phony, so unaware of the authentic mission of the church, that they must be looked upon with saddened despair, if not with outright opposition and disdain. Anyone who has worked in the leadership of the institutional church today will readily recognize this viewpoint as common, persistent, and articulate among some of our best ecclesiastical leadership.

Such an attitude is understandable, inasmuch as it is clear that institutional Christianity has often been introverted, self-congratulatory, and often even hostile and defensive toward precisely the imaginative forms of ministry most promising for the genuine renewal of the church.

The deeper issue, however, has to do with the very doctrine and nature of the church, and not merely with finding an easy way out of our particular institutional predicament—raising budgets, the crisis in authority, reparations, recruiting ministers, etc. There are compelling theological (not just pragmatic and organizational) reasons for affirming the inevitably local and institutional character of the church. A person is not fully serious about Christian existence unless he is willing to work within just those present, given, corporate church structures which are inadequate and need a basic revolution.

Precisely those individuals who have the most legitimate and penetrating complaints against the present phoniness of the church, who have struggled sincerely and futilely to communicate with the existing church of our fathers, are being called to understand these recalcitrant institutional realities against which they currently protest as a manifestation and expression of the historic Christian tradition, albeit fragmented and diseased, but nevertheless participating in the mystery of God's ministry in and for the world.

We are searching for a more vital rapprochement than we have yet achieved between the revolutionary forces at work for church renewal and the common, ordinary, garden-variety institutional church. They need each other. They should not be as far apart as they presently seem to be. What seems to be emerging as a bitter battle between two camps might more profitably become a joint constructive effort between two views of the church which certainly need each other's judgment, criticism, and strength.

There is a comic tendency in theology to regard as an intolerable embarrassment the fact that the church is an institution.[4] It looks rather bad that the church must resort to the same kinds of organizational gimmicks and sociological structures as banks and bureaucrats and bandmasters. It seems as if the church should be able to do something better than calculate budgets, raise money, fight elections, debate according to parliamentary rules, handle public relations, etc. That looks bad.

Why? Because we are constantly tempted to misunderstand the church as if it were a disembodied, nonhistorical community. *Our problem is in the very doctrine of the church, and the fundamental weakness is our misunderstanding of the visibility of the church.* That is *our* problem. It is at heart a theological problem. It is not merely an administrative or funding problem, or some trick of fate in which forces outside the church have put it in this predicament. It is essentially a doctrinal failure: We have not learned to think of the church as an embodied community.[5]

Many people believe not only that they can get along as Christians quite well without the church but also that any institutional embodiment of Christian community is itself a disastrous distortion of what the church should be. It is not clear how the nature of the church as an actual community might be conceived in the minds of the anti-institutionalists. One suspects that it might turn out to be something like a group therapy session. Even in the sphere of group therapy, however, the dimension of responsible commitment to others is being stressed as a persistent dimension of the healing process. The willingness to engage in continuing structures and processes of community-building and enduring covenant relationships is increasingly regarded by many secular therapists as essential to the very core of the healing relationship.[6] Group therapy itself is becoming essentially a corporate commitment of a group of people to help each other to become responsible. So those who vaguely appeal to therapy as a model for genuine community might be rather surprised themselves at what is happening on the growing edge of therapy today in its decisive turn toward corporate accountability as the basis for health.

Our essential theological perplexity is that we cannot fathom how Christ can have a body. We cannot understand how the love of God can be present in the *flesh!* The theological problem of the institutional church is directly analogous to our theological dilemma with the incarnation. Many of us cannot really buy or even seriously grasp the notion that God embodies himself in time or eventfully participates in history. That is precisely our problem with the institutional church. Idealistically we would prefer to think of the church in a dehistorized sense as some future possibility, or as an idea in our minds, rather than a community of warm-bodied human beings.

Thus all the folderol we see going on in the church on the corner is so far from our idealizations about it that we are always (by definition!) disappointed with the church we see! Even the bare possibility that the church *can* exist in history seems to be a disappointment to our idealized romanticisms.

The dogmatic dilemma is as old as docetism, the second-century view which proposed that the Christ was not a bodily presence in history but a sort of imitation body, that God did not really enflesh himself; he only *appeared* to be a body but really was not. The early church battled that notion vigorously. The Chalcedonian formula showed the determination of the church not to get trapped in a dehistorized Christology, while the catholicizing direction showed the determination of the church not to get trapped in a dehistorized ecclesiology. But these two developments move hand in hand: if we cannot conceive of Christ as embodied in time, we probably cannot conceive of the church as embodied in time.

On the other hand, a serious doctrine of incarnation is going to necessitate a serious ecclesiology, i.e., some sort of continuing historical embodiment of the charisma of Christ.[7]

Ex-churchman Charles Davis is correct to point out that institutional structures themselves embody and imply some sort of understanding of truth. Admittedly, if the structures of the church do not embody the meaning of the Christian faith, then the Christian must make some realistic critical response to that false embodiment. But that does not necessarily mean one must abandon the church just because the structures in which it is embodied are imperfect. It might rather mean that one enters those structures all the more deliberately and vigorously, as did the monastic movement in the medieval period, or the Reformation in the sixteenth century, to search for a more adequate embodiment of Christian mission and community. It might mean that we would engage even more deliberately in institutional reconstruction so that the structures themselves could be reformulated.

Even Davis does not recommend that all others leave the church as he has done, since "some of the structures are capable of adaptation." Although for some persons, conscience will require "creative disaffiliation" from denominational structures, "for others it need not do so. They will find sufficient freedom and scope for honest and sincere Christian living and mission within formal membership of their Church. The renewal and reorganization of the Christian Church will be achieved by people working from either direction, from without as well as from within the present Church structures."[8]

"My objection therefore is not against institutions as such. It does not arise from a prejudice that all institutions are impersonal and inimical to persons. What I hold is that the present social structure of the church is no longer a living institution, in as much as it no longer adequately embodies Christian experience. . . . It clashes with the contemporary Christian consciousness and cannot serve as the expression and vehicle of Christian commitment in the modern world. Since it survives as an empty shell from a past age, the attempt to keep it in being is inevitably inimical to persons."[9]

Is the church establishment really ready to hear Davis' "question of conscience"? What if the institutional structures of the church themselves prevent people from expressing Christian love and from being themselves? What if they make people immature and scar the human psyche? Do not these persons have the right to reject such an institution? The answer certainly must be yes. He has not only the right but the responsibility to reject those dimensions of the institution which are harmful and obstructive to authentic humanity. If persons have received psychological damage from the abuses of bad institutional structures, then it is only understandable and meaningful that those structures be rejected. One would hope that they would leave the church, and wish them well in it, if their lives could be mended and more fully lived outside the church. But this still leaves many questions unanswered. If the church is this obstructive, what responsibilities do we have to try to reform it? Can it be reformed by withdrawing from it? Is it adequately and objectively described by those who have been most deeply hurt by it?

Just as it is incorrect to judge the validity of democracy by its abuses, so it is unfair to judge the church exclusively by its worst examples. The idea of democracy is not to be rejected just because the Mississippi legislature abuses democracy. The federal judiciary is not to be dismissed or abolished because of the inappropriate actions of one of its members. Marxist thought is not completely false just because of the inequities and paranoia of Stalinism. Likewise the case of the church is not finally to be judged by looking at the Rasputins and Hitlers and Hargises, but also by looking at the Tolstoys and Bonhoeffers and John Twenty-thirds. Where there have been abuses, as there certainly have, there have always in time been prophets and reformers who have tried to correct the abuses, without denying the apostolic continuity of the larger Christian tradition.

What would have happened to the church of the medieval period if Francis of Assisi had taken the advice of the necro-ecclesiologists to leave the church; or to the Reformation if Calvin had not worked hard at institutional reconstruction of the visible church; or to pietism if Walter Rauschenbusch had just quit the church and become a Marxist revolutionary; or to the racist church if Martin Luther King, Jr., had abandoned his ministry? In each case both church and society would have been less, not more, creative. Instead, each of these ecclesial revolutionaries chose to work within the delivered structures to reform their inadequacies, not merely to condemn and abandon them in the midst of their shortsightedness.

CHAPTER 2

The Institutional Church
and Revolutionary Change

Among ecclesiastical bureaucrats, where one would least expect it, the "institutional church" has become a four-letter word. It is a curious season of history in which "the establishment" is everybody's whipping boy, and the established church has become the scapegoat even of the most established churchmen. It must be sunspots. Any second-rate Chautauqua speaker can flail "the institutional church" and warm the hearts of his hearers with gratifying results.

In an era in which institutional ecclesia is almost universally maligned (except by those who are desperately defending it precisely in its present limited forms), we are searching for a new grasp of the embodiment of Christian mission in visible forms. We do not intend uncritically to "Uncle Tom" present church structures, or provide a scented apologia for *all* the odoriferous ecclesial forms we have inherited from twenty centuries of trial and error at being Christians, or to put on rose-colored glasses and congratulate a phony church for a job poorly done, but we do intend to try to provide a theological foundation for renewed emphasis in the building of institutional continuity in the Christian tradition. The weight of our argument falls toward the minority viewpoint that the church, wherever it exists, is always embodied in some institutional structure. If the church by definition is a body, it therefore demands some sort of deliberate organizational embodiment.

Our initial thesis: Far from being inescapably dehumanizing (as they are often conceived), institutional structures are the necessary matrix of the humanizing process. Far from being inevitably stultifying to human freedom, institutional processes are the necessary milieu out of which human freedom springs and develops. The well-conceived institutional structure may be celebrated by the Christian community as joyfully as the individual freedom that thrives within it.

Institutional structures are programming devices to free us as individuals from the endless, frustrating process of trial-and-error experimentation in the construction of human environments. They enable us to bank on the funded resources of human social experience. Sociological inquiry into the process of social legitimation has helped us to understand that we need not idolatrize institutions in order to regard them as functionally valuable.[1] We are free as modern men to receive institutional traditions, remake them with joy, dancing with gratitude for their stored human achievements.

"Institutional church" here means the empirical church in its visible, organizational forms—the church we see. It is the existing, experienced church, the church as it ordinarily presents itself, the church on the corner, the ordinary garden variety of parish structure, both in its local manifestation and in its supralocal hierarchical structures. We are searching for a fresh interpretation of the organized church. Rather than pursuing a strictly scientific, descriptive statement of the church as an institution, we are instead attempting to grasp a theological understanding of the church visible, with its given institutional forms and delivered traditions.[2]

The body of Christ must be embodied. That involves

organizational structure. Consequently the task of institution-building, organizational management, and administration is never an optional addendum on the agenda of the missioning church but is elemental to the very reality of the church as a historic community.

Ordinarily theological treatises on the church dwell at great length upon the nonempirical, nonorganizational dimensions of the church: its holiness, its catholicity, etc. Theology has regrettably left the empirical church to sociology and church administration. Our critical need now is to reverse that pattern: to provide a serious theological statement on the visibility of the church, and to explore its consequences.

Definitions of institutions by sociologists vary widely. This diversity itself is an indication of the complexity of institutional phenomena. Certain theorists who emphasize society as a system of action describe institutions as "established patterns of action," while others emphasize the normative (rule-setting) character of institutionalization as a means of social control. Others speak of institutions as "patterns of roles," "social habits which are systematized," or "organizations of collective activities."[3]

A more complex definition is offered by J. O. Hertzler (who has studied institutions more exhaustively than any American sociologist), who defines a social institution as "(1) a set of chartered and sanctioned behavioral directives and expectations, both of a positive and prohibitive nature, (2) expressed by the individuals involved as patterned roles for the various social positions and situations, and (3) aided by a complex of conformity-producing social usages and procedures and implementing social organizations, symbolic materials and, in most instances, physical equipment, whereby human beings systematically satisfy some basic need or related needs."[4] In their chief historic forms, Christian communities have always exhibited the components of this definition. There are, however, a num-

ber of hard words in that definition: "behavioral directives," "conformity-producing," "patterned roles," etc.
These images which we often associate with the restric-
tion of human freedom, we will argue, may actually become the enablers of human freedom.

Whichever interpretation of the institutionalizing process one might find most persuasive, virtually all sociologists agree that some sort of institutions are necessary and
essential to society. It would be impossible to conceive of
human social achievements without institutions. That
might seem such an obvious truism it would be unnecessary to state, if it were not for a great morass of popular
opinion which holds the opposite, that institutional
existence, wherever it is found, is inevitably dehumanizing and corrupt, and that only the individual is pure and
undefiled. In the sociological literature, however, the
crucial question is not whether we will have institutions
but what kind of institutions we shall construct and how
adequately they will meet our human and social needs.[5]

Institutions emerge because certain needs can be satisfied only through social organization. As soon as any col-
lection of people develop a system of social relationships
and coordinate social roles, however elementary they may
be, they have created an institution, whether they are
teen-age motorcyclists or prison inmates or aborigines or
lovers. "When any new type of relationship or interpersonal activity becomes recurrent and essential, it must be
institutionalized. The only alternative would be to invent
adequate rules and procedures for the particular relationship or function on the spot and at the moment; and this
few individuals or groups are capable of doing."[6]

Institutions are the means by which human beings
order and correlate their activities. We could not have
this particular society without these particular institutions. Institutions function in a regulative role as means
of social control. It is by means of institutions that we

learn to reshape our subjective impulses and individual energies into socially acceptable forms of behavior.

Institutions function as means of conserving particular memories and patterns of behavior from generation to generation. Armed with the memory that the institution provides and guarantees, one enters into the present with a perceptual framework. It channels behavior so individuals can know more readily how to meet the new. Thus the white line down the highway shows us where to drive. It simplifies the decision-making process so that each time we meet a car, we do not have to stop and discuss how to pass. That is how an institution functions.

Far from being against all instinctual or biological urges or drives, institutions provide structured means of satisfying erotic drives in ways that are not destructive to the larger social organism. The institutionalizing of behavioral patterns saves the individual an incalculable amount of time so that he does not have to discover new criteria in each new situation that arises. They supply him with a fund of solutions that have been remembered and traditioned to the present. They make it unnecessary for us to reorganize society every morning in order to get breakfast or the morning paper. In this sense we owe our institutions a great debt.

Institutions also have a "time-binding function." Individuals come and go, and do not guarantee the continuity of values in history. Only transgenerational institutions can embody historical continuities. Insofar as the church has continuity, it is achieved through the wisdom of institution-building. It is by means of institutions that the meanings of the past are traditioned into the present, become organized and reshaped in the light of experience, and, it is hoped, handed on to the future. So there is a sense in which the achievements of a society are essentially seen in the achievements of its institutions. "The great recognized values in the social life of men are em-

bodied in their institutions and through them are safe-
guarded and transmitted to posterity. What is not found
in institutions is essentially individualistic, or eccentric,
or momentary, and not comprised in the common life.
Hence, a society's culture is largely a summation of its
institutions, and its institutions are largely an embodiment of its culture."[7]

Our problem in any discussion of institutions, however, lies not with formal sociological definition, but
rather with ordinary language usage. For in popular
parlance, the terms "institution" and "institutionalization" are often used in a pejorative sense, as if they were
inevitably opposed to freedom, charisma, spirit, and self-
determination. It is often assumed that by their very
definition institutions are dehumanizing. Conditioned by
our frontier past, our popular language has tended to
define social institutions in such a way that they appear
intrinsically against rather than for man and his freedom.
This serious deficiency in popular definition reflects our
predisposition to an outdated individualism.[8]

"Of course, the very word 'institution' has to English
ears of my generation unfortunate associations," says
British ethicist Leslie Paul. "In my youth it was used
pretty exclusively about places to be stayed away from
at all costs; where today we talk of 'homes,' 'hospitals,'
'centers,' 'schools,' then we talked of mental institutions,
reform institutions, poor law institutions, and the like.
The sentence of death on a neighbour in my boyhood
was the whisper: 'He's been put away in an institution.'
It meant that one would never see him again in the land
of the living. The institutions had much in common:
architecturally they were grim Victorian blocks with echo-
ing corridors smelling of cabbage: they looked like prisons
or fortresses. Socially, visitors were not encouraged: the
communities were enclosed ones."[9]

To define institutions as "conformity-creating mechanisms" or "instruments for guaranteeing social control" creates a preconception of the institution as an imprisoning reality instead of a liberating reality. Against this general trend, I would like to argue that more often than not institutional structures are liberating realities, and that, surprisingly enough, *it is precisely by means of the strategies of social control that they become liberating.*

Without attempting here to enter into a complex discussion of the criteria by which we may judge institutions to be better or worse, we would propose this as a heuristic hypothesis. It is through the grooving or programming of individual behavior that social institutions render the individual such a great service, providing him with the remembered corporate experience of generations, freeing him from the painful and hazardous trial-and-error process through which human history has already once suffered. It would be absurd and anti-anthropological to propose to do away with human institutions. Admittedly not all institutions are equally liberating. New England theocracy, Victorian morality, or the feudal economy might serve as examples of relatively oppressive institutional structures. And even in those cases it could be argued that the oppression suffered was to be preferred to sheer social chaos or total structurelessness. Certainly in most cases reasonable men have found that some institution is better than none.[10] Bad as corrupt institutions may be, history has found them more congenial than anarchic nativism. Even amid the revolutionary process of destroying one institution, as our forefathers destroyed a certain form of colonialism in 1776, they were quite clear that the better alternative to a bad institution was not anarchy but a better institutional procedure.

With all our social skills, we have not yet developed the freedom to reshape institutional forms without hating and maligning the past out of which they grew distorted. We seem to have temporarily lost the capacity to celebrate the brilliant achievements of our historic institutions while we amend their weaknesses. We have not yet learned the delicate game of creative interaction between tradition and renewal, institution and charisma. In refusing to involve ourselves creatively in this delicate mechanism of social adjustment, we lose something of ourselves as historical beings. For we are human beings who have grown out of particular histories, and who are charged with remaking history. Aware or not, however, we are conditioned by our institutional environments. The question is: Are we clever enough to change them into better institutional environments?

CHAPTER 3

The Search for a New Establishment

The World Council of Churches study on institutionalism and unity, which was presented by the Commission on Faith and Order in 1961, called for increased theological investigation of the institutional factors that promote and hinder mission and unity, and for sustained debate on the relation of charisma and order, visibility and invisibility, continuity and discontinuity, and for the development of a theology of institutions. It is unfortunate that a decade has gone by and that call has never been answered seriously.[1] This is regrettable, since during the same time we have been caught in a whirlwind of historic change that has called for creative institutional reformulation, but we have not been in a mood to think institutionally. We have been thinking ideologically and abstractly, but not in terms of the difficult process of rebuilding the body of Christ in the light of our knowledge of sociological processes and of our new theological understanding of the Christian mission.

The World Council study on *The Old and the New in the Church* correctly argued: "It is in keeping with our belief in the Christian incarnation to affirm that the church through all these institutional dimensions, though in varying degrees, is embedded and involved in all conditions of society and history. Conversely, it is equally true that all these institutional patterns—even to financial campaigns and bureaucratic regulations—possess theological dignity, though again in varying degrees."[2]

In all of our talk of the need for institutional continuity, we must not pretend that there are no urgent requirements for decisive, radical change.[3] If by "a revolution" we mean turning things completely over, as a revolution of a wheel is a complete turn, then we are living in revolutionary times. Many elements of the social environment are turning completely over.[4]

We are witnessing the destruction of many old patterns that we have long associated with the church. To some generations it is given to build. To others, it is given to suffer the destruction of older orders. Our fathers' generation was essentially a builders' generation, but in many ways ours is a generation in which we are watching the destruction and deterioration of much that they built. It is a part of our historical givenness, and therefore a gift of God, that we are beholding the destruction of old orders, built on weak foundations that never had the promise of long-term service to man.[5] One doesn't expect a cracker-box house to last a thousand years. So it is with certain structures that we have inherited. Just because they are associated with the frontier church, and with its vigorous history and institutional forms, that is no reason to feel sentimental about them. We need to learn to rejoice even amid the destruction of many of these forms. This is not to urge a macabre attitude of cynical rejoicing over the collapse of deteriorating institutions, but rather the constructive task of rebuilding on the ashes of destruction and learning to assess the meaning of the destruction itself.

We are now experiencing the collapse of denominational identities. We may have loved our denominations, and felt a tug of loyalty to them, but that is beside the point now. We could not maintain these structures even if we tried. The denominational structures are simply on their way out. History can no longer tolerate a divided church. The structures are cracking and crumbling. That is difficult for us to adjust to. The whole ecclesial mechanism is organized along denominational lines. It is difficult to rebuild toward ecumenical institutions. It is not so hard to develop an ecumenical *idea,* or to think ecumenical thoughts, or to have ecumenical discussions—but to construct ecumenical *institutions*—that is much more difficult. It takes a lot of imagination. Yet this is the challenge of the church in our times—to find means of developing ecumenical institutional continuity so that the gospel can be mediated to the evolving world amid its massive changes, yet without total cultural absorption by that world.

We older radicals now in our thirties have worked hard and long for this day. We have planned and strategized and hoped for the time when basic breakthroughs would be eminently possible, when the old leadership would fall of its own weight, when the massive power and organizational resources of a pragmatic generation of institution builders would grow tired and senile and yield to new initiatives. As young churchmen, we had hoped to be ready for this moment with a well-hewn concept of the church's mission and a well-conceived plan for actualizing that mission.

We have come just to that promising period of breakthrough, but we are now even more than ever unprepared to meet it. The irony is that just at the decisive moment of opportunity, we are more hung up than ever with our old disease of institutional cynicism. Like losing the final battle while the enemy is in full retreat, we now seem ready to throw in the towel on the institutional church. Precisely at this moment of unexcelled opportunity we find ourselves less motivated than ever to engage in the patient tasks of institutional reconstruction, in the hardheaded sense of building better budgets, taking seriously nominating committees, developing long-range institutional planning, etc. We are not geared for that. We are only in the mood for mouthing platitudes. We enjoy more the sheer luxury of bemoaning the present phoniness of the establishment, now that we clearly have the opportunity. We would prefer to be safely *outside* the forum of human decision and responsibility. We may not be as politically astute or motivated as the noises we make would lead some to believe. We prefer the riskless refuge of a cynical criticism that lacks genuine self-criticism. We want to gripe about our lousy situation, but do not really want to participate in the painful, slow process of patient reconstruction of church and society that would embody some of the ideals we have been mouthing and placarding. That is our moral quandary. We may be as hypocritical as any generation that ever struggled quixotically against hypocrisy.

It is this cynical mentality against which we must struggle, both in ourselves and in others. If we fail to see these inherited structures as they actually are, i.e., as extremely vulnerable and ready for change, then it is our misperception that is at fault. The establishment we have safely enjoyed blasting is now inviting our responsible participation in many ways that we are often too adolescent or paranoic even to recognize.

When the tension between tradition and renewal is obliterated, as I believe it often is in much pseudo-revolutionary action, a serious loss results for the human community. The malignant weakness of simplistic calls for radical change is that they are never radical enough. They are too wordy and superficial. They are often not really concerned with the actual administration of justice, but merely with abstract slogans about justice.

Although the conservative mentality may lack a sensitized conscience, and often is more concerned with its own vested interest than with others' needs, its one great strength is its wary suspiciousness of simplistic solutions to complex human problems, its tendency to regard overstated optimism with extreme caution, and its unwillingness to buy just anybody's impromptu proposal for the new order. *Caveat emptor* ("Let the buyer beware") is the model not only of conservative business but of conservative politics.

More urgently needed today than jaded conservatism, however, is what might be called a "conserving radicalism," which is committed to conserving the basis of revolutionary action. Such a mutating conservatism would focus its attention upon the hardheaded, pragmatic implementation of new ideas and programs for human betterment without paying the unconscionable price of the obliteration of man's past achievements.

When the élan of pseudo-revolutionary radicalism is abroad, as Eric Hoffer has pointed out, there is often little to be constructively achieved: "When hopes and dreams are loose in the streets, it is well for the timid to lock doors, shutter windows and lie low until the wrath has passed. For there is often a monstrous incongruity between the hopes, however noble and tender, and the action which follows them. It is as if ivyed maidens and garlanded youths were to herald the four horsemen of the apocalypse."[6]

We are now undeniably whirling in the maelstrom of such revolutionary transition. Moltmann may be right, that the utopian who presses so radically for futurity and rejects totally the old, does indeed perform a significant function,[7] but his function is painfully limited and must be exceptionally well timed to special historical conditions. I am seeing the role of the revolutionary these days much more in a functional sense: to awaken the massive central body of decision-making into conscience and the need for change. But from a broader perception of history, the revolutionary stance is in itself inadequate and must come to institutionalize its charisma if it is to make any enduring sort of contribution to history. We have reason to be suspicious of messianic pretensions that hold out great promise without being able to deliver actual change. That is why I question whether Moltmann's theology of hope is a truly hopeful theology since it tends to flee the hard reality of the present and focus its consciousness exclusively and imaginatively upon the future.

In his shrewd description of "the true believer" who joins mass movements aimed at immediate, total social change, Hoffer has accurately described many of the more volatile elements of revolutionary utopianism, pious or otherwise.[8] The time has come for the conserving radicals (radicals who wish to conserve the basis for revolutionary action) to repudiate and challenge the sincerity of absolutist revolutionary strategies as a betrayal of their own most exalted intentions.

If a theology of revolution means the baptizing of a strategy for social change that bombs, burns, and genocidally demolishes the past, it surely must be repudiated by every Christian committed to the love of the neighbor.[9] We, too, are for change, at all deliberate speed, but no reasonable man could applaud a total uncritical annihilation of man's past social achievements. If that is what revolution means, it must not only be repudiated but fought to the last barricade with the utmost determination. The renewing church will thrive in the midst of a responsible dialogue between tradition and renewal, but must never become captive to a concept of renewal that obliterates, disembowels, and annihilates tradition, nor by any view of tradition that archaically imprisons the spirit of renewal.

With my friends in the University Christian Movement, I have spent many long evenings bemoaning the deplorable conditions of the institutional church, especially with respect to its lack of interest or investment in the campus ministry. The university, we complained, had become a fourth-rate priority of the church's institutional planning. We joined together in an enthusiastic chorus of well-deserved damnation of the institutional church.

As time went by, through a long process of agitation and hard work, we tried to awaken the institutional church to the urgent need for a relevant campus ministry. With the cooperation of the awakening establishment, we made an intensive study of the mission of the church on campus, its funding, its ministry, and we made our reports. To the surprise of everyone, they were convincing to the establishment, and soon to our astonishment we began to see more money coming into the student movement from the environing churches. We began to raise our professional standards, intensify our mission, improve our equipment, etc. Soon we found ourselves faced with establishment-type problems, trying to allocate funds to numerous projects, all of which we found relatively important for the church's mission.

The question arises: What were we working for in that earlier period when we were struggling so desperately against the "institutional church"? Answer: Precisely for *a better institutionalization* of the campus ministry.[10] What we wanted was a more adequate structure for professional leadership, financial support, etc. Moral: The most bitter opponents of the establishment are often not quite ready to see that what they really want is a piece of the establishment, and to be more appropriately institutionalized themselves.

Radical politics often looks radically anti-establishment, but if the radical ideals were brought to life in actual social constructs (e.g., if the vision of the Port Huron statement[11] were enacted into law), the authentic radicals would be energetically creating a new establishment, hammering out new institutional forms. This is obvious to anyone who thinks seriously about social change, but it is unfortunate that it is not recognized as obvious by those who enjoy anticipating the funeral of the establishment without serious self-awareness of their legitimate moral concern to displace it with another, better, establishment.

Is it true that some institutionalization, even though corrupt, is better than anarchy? How dehumanizing is anarchy? This is difficult to imagine, since most civilized men have never experienced it except in remotely fragmented forms. During the New York garbage strike, in a matter of hours garbage was knee-deep. Just such a mundane problem dramatizes the importance of complex social ordering and efficient bureaucratic organization. We must find some way of disposing of our garbage, and if we do not have a social mechanism to dispose of garbage, we literally are not free to walk in our streets.

So we are not standing against freedom in emphasizing the importance of institutions, but for a freedom that is enabled through social organization. Freedom has too often been romanticized by people who think of it in purely individualistic terms. We have come to an end of the spirit of permissiveness in modern American society. However delicious permissiveness may have been, or however much we may have enjoyed participating in it, it is now over. The deaths of Martin Luther King, Jr., and Robert F. Kennedy have abruptly punctuated its demise. Oswald, Ray, and Sirhan have painfully taught us of the end of permissiveness. They embody a radical individual antinomianism that does not recognize the social contract, nor acknowledge the debt we owe to each other by the very fact of our being human beings.

Institutional structures need to be constantly criticized and changed in accordance with changing historical conditions. Yet it is nothing but the wildest optimism that would imagine that we could do away with institutions totally in the church or anywhere else.[12] Yet just this kind of messianic individualism is abroad today in a society whose advanced institutions of civil liberties have provided an arena for it to be heard, protected, and broadcast in living color.

Part II

THE UNDERGROUND:
A CAUTIOUS CRITIQUE

CHAPTER 4

On Quitting the Church

Why are sincere churchmen, from time to time, sorely tempted to give up on the institutional church? The rich term "mendacity," as used by Tennessee Williams in *Cat on a Hot Tin Roof*, seems to get to the heart of the quandary. Mendacity means living a lie, a life-style burdened with self-deception. Partly because we profess such high hopes for humanity, churchmen often lead lives deeply trapped in mendacity. Mendacity is constantly seen in the effort to legitimize inauthentic structures and indefensible beliefs.[1] It is seen in the horrifying distance between words and deeds, doctrine and action, liturgy and love.

When churchmen in the name of Christ whitewash obviously unjust social structures, clothing tyranny and oppression with the alleged "will of God," we should expect sensitive people to quit the church. That the church is a tranquilizer is a classic Marxist critique, but it nonetheless remains a plausible and penetrating judgment that churchmen should never forget. It is undeniable that churchmen often use religion to validate and rationalize their own political and social interests, using God-language to "legitimize" the most atrocious actions of war, genocide, racism, and tribalism.[2]

Some will experience our entire issue as misplaced. Traditionalists, who are alienated from the emerging generation and willing to let the Christian community rise or fall with the destinies of the passing generation, will wonder why the question should even be pursued. The futuric types, on the other hand, may bring to the issue no honest concern for continuity in the Christian tradition. Neither of these two opposite groups will experience existentially the disturbing problem to which we are addressing ourselves.

But there are some who behold the modern world, yearning for a significant embrace with it, and a celebration of it, yet with a profound awareness that precisely this world stands in urgent need of the wisdom of the Christian tradition and of some concrete institutional embodiment of the Christian community and of the life of Christian love.

We cannot evade the burdensome character of this question for those of us who experience it. It is a heavy, demanding question for those who are equally concerned for both the modern world and the reality of the church.[3] We experience the immense gulf between Christ and modernity. The gulf will be bridged by only visible, sociologically credible institutions. It cannot be done by relying on sheer spontaneous, unstructured, sporadic charisma without any deliberate concern for historic continuity.

Simultaneously we are aware of the future with its amazing promise for increased humanization, but also of its violent prospects for dehumanization. We are aware that we are committed to a tradition which, however great it may have been or should be, has lost its plausibility, and has been identified by many of the emerging generation as one of the villains in the struggle for a new future.[4] It is to this emerging generation that we are really reaching out. It is with them in mind that we raise so urgently the question of the relation of tradition and renewal.

There is no need now to resurrect the already over-worked syndrome of cheap criticism of the church. Nor do we wish to recapitulate the valuable ecclesiological work done by others.[5] The extensive research that has been done on the lay apostolate, the mission of the church to the world, secular spirituality, and the history of ecclesiology need not be repeated and should be often consulted.[6] What has not been adequately stated, however, is why the church needs institutional continuity, and how that continuity can be achieved in the midst of the revolution which is our times.

An astonishing number of loyal churchmen, who previously have never even remotely conceived of the possibility of leaving the church, now are struggling to decide why they should be committed to it. We are addressing persons who now have or have had some serious commitment to the church, yet a commitment that is now undergoing severe strains amid the current challenge to the church's credibility. We are addressing the wavering, the uncertain, ambivalent churchman who has not yet firmly made up his mind about whether the Christian enterprise, as expressed in its current institutions, is worth his time and money and trust.

We have in mind not merely religious professionals, but churchmen of all sorts, young and old, lay and clergy, liberal and conservative, who suspect that the church is worth working for, but who have not articulated for themselves why, and who are now torn by doubt concerning its current institutional viability. We are reaching out for churchmen who are frightened, awed, cowed, or threatened by the newness of the modern world, and wonder how the church can survive, and whether it should.

For many, the church has every appearance of belonging to a day gone by. It seems to be so much a part of past eras: medieval, monarchic eras, or more recently, the era of individualistic, narrow, puritanical, bourgeois society. It seems too deeply indebted to these viewpoints ever to escape the trap. It is against the church's apparent master, business culture, and middle-class morality, that the younger generation is rebelling today. If one has clearly imprinted in his mind the association that church belongs to the old, while science and technology belong to the new humanity, then he just feels, "Why bother?" toward the church. Why even worry about it? That is something parents are hung up on. It is not a real question. For many in the emerging generation, it is of no concern; they have already quit the church. They quit it when they realized that the church was an appendix of a senile and deteriorating Western culture. The image of the church as deteriorating belongs to a much larger social perception that Western culture as a whole is deteriorating.

The Freudian revolution has tended to imprint on our consciousness the view that all premodern societies were sexually repressive, and that therefore the only way to become a human being is to cast off these repressive, past modes of social existence. It is with this kind of mentality that the church has become tragically, but decisively, identified in the emerging mind. Add to that a Marxist interpretation of history, which sees history as in a revolutionary process moving toward a totally new form of social organization, while religion plays the role of consistent apologist for an order of things that has already been passed by. The tendency to want to quit the church is understandably a part of a much larger tendency to want to quit anything that has any strong kinship with the past world.[7]

As a whole this generation which we are watching grow is an innovative, promising, resourceful generation. But we cannot really say that this generation has adequately grasped the promise and possibility of historic Christianity contributing significantly to that emerging world for which they are hoping. Rather, it tends to perceive the church as an opponent, an obstacle, a drag on the momentum of history. People quit the church because they would rather do more important things than spend their time in busywork, in routinized structures and archaic meanings which they suspect are actually opposed to the true interests of mankind.

Theologians like myself have the overwhelming problem of making plausible these structures to which we have committed ourselves, and to which we have been assigned some sort of guardian role. At least it is imperative that we try to show historically how things got this way, and try to provide some systematic, consistent explanation of the inner reality and concern of the church, even if its external embodiment is quite inadequate, and to give some prospectus for its potential engagement with the emerging world.

Now we shift our focus to ask: What is it that keeps drawing us back to the church? Despite all these persuasive criticisms, why are we drawn back toward the church's message, its liturgy, its history, its proclamation, its corporate life? What about the church is lovable despite all its unloveliness?

What constrains our continuing commitment to it? Essentially the gospel: That the One who gives us life has made himself known as the One who loves us in the midst of our sin, who shares our life with us, who participates in history, and takes the burden of humanity upon himself. This love will not let us go. It is the constraining power in the life of the church which will not leave us alone in our human stratagems.

There is a plentiful supply of churchmen who are frightened by the prospects of the revolutionary future, who cannot envision anything in that future for the church, who can only respond to futurity with a sense of defensive dread. To such persons, we are not merely suggesting that the church grimly should grit its teeth and try to manage for the next five years or possibly twenty. Rather, we will explore the possibility that these times constitute a unique opportunity for the Christian community.

Our hypothesis is this: Never has there been a time in which it has been more exciting to be a person whose life has been shaped by the Christian memory in confronting the need and possibility of the world than today.

Christianity is a worldwide community. Rare among human institutions, it has a two-millennium history. It is not going to disappear tomorrow. More Christians are alive today than at any previous time in the church's history. More persons today receive the Sacraments and hear the preaching of the word than ever before. With improved means of historical research, we now know more about the Biblical witness and historical Christian tradition than any previous generation.

It hardly seems fitting for us to waste away in despair over the alleged loneliness and isolation of the church from the secularizing process when the church itself has been one of the progenitors of secularization.[8] In fact, there is no room at all for despair for those who trust in God's future, and who expectantly await the future as the arena of the self-disclosure of the One who gives us life.

Let us delight in breathing the air of modernity, in wandering the streets of youth culture, in exploring new land, in settling the new frontiers of emerging culture.[9] These times call us not merely to congratulate ourselves on our participation in the building of past societies, however laudable or damnable, but to see this current society as the embryo of a new mutation of man toward which the church is called to be present in mission and service, and to create models for genuine humanity and community.

The question is not merely how to keep cool amid revolutionary change. It is how to negotiate that change constructively. How do we catch the Molotov cocktails and refashion them into something humanizing? It is noteworthy that the Molotov cocktail is composed of the same elements as the ignition process of a motor: fuel and fire. It is curious that this symbol of destruction concentrates the elements for constructive change in our society. No automobile could move without gasoline and spark plugs. But the fuel and fire must be geared to a productive, rationalized mechanism in order to do anything but destroy. That is our problem: How do we take the elements of the Molotov cocktail and do something constructive with them?

Chapter 5

Questions for Subterraneans

The underground church deserves a thoughtful and respectful reply. Thoughtful, because there is much being said by the underground that established churchmen must learn to hear, and hear quickly. Respectful, because of the underground church's manifest courage, hope for renewal, and concern for the poor.

The underground has found the inherited structures impossible. It has decided to work covertly, to go outside these structures, in order truly to celebrate the gospel and serve humanity. The underground image of the church resonates with so many sensitive persons that it can hardly be brushed off as a "passing phase." It strikes such a deep chord that we cannot doubt that it contains many elements of unmistakable authenticity, despite its tendencies toward romanticism and sometimes cynicism.

Charles Davis, the eminent British ex-Roman Catholic theologian who quit the church in 1966, has expressed his disappointment that his critics have not seriously responded to the basis upon which he left the church, namely, as a question of faith. It was not a matter of tactics or a personal clash with authority. "I did not justify my defection as a forceful means of provoking reform; I did not set out to strike a blow for the break-up of the present churches and the promotion of a new structure

for the embodiment of Christian presence in the world.
. . . For me the basis of any action of reform must be
a true understanding of the Christian faith."[1] It is just
at this point that we wish to join the dialogue. We are
searching for a theology of the visible church and of the
meaning of apostolicity amid revolutionary change.

Charles Davis has called upon those who have remained with the church "clearly and unambiguously to
state the grounds on which they advocate continuing
membership."[2] It is the intention of this essay not only
to state a personal apologia for why one theologian con-
tinues to work within the institution but plausible reasons
why others generally might conscientiously be counseled
to continue a critical and creative participation in the
visible church amid its present predicament and promise.

It is not self-evident why the majority of theologians
who have been nurtured on the same (Tillichian, Bon-
hoefferian, Teilhardian) bread as the underground have
deliberately chosen to stay within the established church
structures. It is ironic that a decision to stay in the church
seems to demand a more thoughtful reply than a decision
to leave. Significantly, it is a more demanding theological
task in our time to write a rationale for working for
change within the traditional church than to write a
Charles Davis farewell.

Only a few theologians have recently attempted this
more difficult task, notably James Dittes and Gregory
Baum.[3] Although a distinct minority in terms of public
expression, this view certainly represents the majority of
theologians and church renewalists. But why is it that
the underground can so readily achieve plausibility, while
the task becomes so burdensome for the majority who
are trying to work responsibly to reformulate the given
structures? That is a subject we will treat later when we
speak of "the moral plausibility of emerging subcultures."
In any case it is evident that a relatively small number

of subterranean spokesmen have captured the attention of the mass media. Perhaps this is because it is always easier to state a clear moral negative than to deal constructively with complex and ambiguous realities.

I respect the deeper loyalties of many who have shaped the underground mentality, notably Charles Davis and Malcolm Boyd. This discussion in no way questions their basic motivation or commitment to the Christian faith. It is merely an attempt to respond to their rejection of the present institutional structures as utterly incapable of significant reform. All I want is the opportunity to account for myself as one who has faced the same question of conscience as Charles Davis did, but answered it in the opposite way. I wish to show that all the morality of this debate does not self-evidently lie on the side of those who "creatively disaffiliate." Rather than attempting to refute Davis, Pike, Boyd, and others who have given up on the present structures, I wish to indicate why there may be substantial reasons for remaining critically loyal to these present inadequate structures as a more hopeful and moral alternative than abandonment. If there is a time for creative disaffiliation, as we must acknowledge, then there must also be a time for creative affiliation.

THE VULNERABILITY OF THE RESISTANCE ANALOGY

Much that Malcolm Boyd is saying about "the underground church" surely must be appreciated by any perceptive observer. "The underground's main task," says Boyd, "is to look *outside* Church structure, to see the people in the world and love them."[4]

This rich image is borrowed from the resistance movement. The assumption is that one must work undercover, resisting a tyrannical establishment that does not allow dissent, such as the Nazi regime, or the Roman Empire against which the early church gathered in catacombs as an underground movement. The image assumes that although the underground has not yet surfaced, it can and will at the right time, and that it bears the true promise of the society in which it is now hiddenly operating as a network of opposition. That is a very powerful image, and a somewhat useful one to certain elements within the renewing church today. It may be an appropriate image in some situations. But as a whole there are basic ambiguities with the underground image which those who employ it sometimes fail to recognize.

Boyd himself seems to be aware of some of the "simplistic naïve entrapments" of the underground image: "self-righteousness, a self-made identification with 'the remnant,' the supposed destruction of institutions . . . pure community versus corrupt perversion of community, and so on."[5] Others who have contributed to his book on *The Underground Church* may not be as aware of these limitations as Boyd thinks, as is evidenced by the fact that all the dangers he enumerates are fully embodied in the book of essays which he edited.

The underground image may become a disastrous rejection of the concept of the *presence* of Christ in the world. The underground image dilutes the fruitful notion of visible Christian presence by thinking of the church as a covert, secret, closed organization.[6]

The underground may find itself hung up on a pietistic self-concern about its own moral integrity, as opposed to actual, effective changes in visible social structures.[7] Another flaw: the minority is always judged to be morally superior to the majority. Smallness is morally better.

The underground seems unconcerned about its own temptation to cultural accommodation, or to what H. R. Niebuhr calls the "synthesist" position of "the Christ of culture."[8] Although Boyd attempts "to preserve the content of the gospel as over against cultural interpretations of it which have come under the captivity of nationalism, colonialism, Puritanism, and Fundamentalism,"[9] he does not always recognize the cultural forms in which the underground itself has become trapped, such as bourgeoisie night life, the radical new left, and popular youth subculture. We may admire forms of Christian cultural accommodation that relate meaningfully to promising subcultures. But in each case the church must ask about the price of conformity.

Peter Berger has shrewdly shown that much subterranean talk, far from being revolutionary, is rather on the whole a new form of culture protestantism. "What would *really* be revolutionary would be to take seriously the beliefs of the New Testament, of the early Christian confessions, or of the 16th century reformers," says Berger. "Norman Vincent Peale, with whose moral positions the 'radicals' disagree so fiercely, differs not one iota from the basic ideological procedure that they themselves employ."[10] To suppose that the underground is trying out something new and lonely is to ignore what has been happening in religion for a decade. "Worker priest experiments, dialogue sermons, jazz liturgies, pop art Jesus figures—one only has to consult the Christmas 1964 issue of *Time* magazine to see that these are anything but the lonely visions of about-to-be-crucified heretics."[11]

The underground church, by its own admission, is often less interested in dialogue than in conflict per se. According to its own literature, it works covertly, without open disclosure, against consensus and discussion. In contrasting himself with the institutional church, one underground spokesman[12] made the following astonishing two-column contrast:

Institutional Church	*Underground Church*
uniting	dividing
openness	covertness
consensus	conflict
trust	suspicion

persuasion	manipulation
flight	fight
generalization	specificity
discussion	action
full communication	selective communication
high visibility	low visibility

These are not my associations, but are proposed by Layton Zimmer as criteria for his own "underground church." A careful study of these word associations is extremely revealing with respect to the almost paranoiac self-conception of the underground. It is clear that the institutional church with all its resistance is much more interested in dialogue than is this concept of the underground. The underground intends to be divisive. It is disinterested in consensus. Since it deals covertly with an elite ingroup, suspiciousness is the hallmark of all its dealings, even of those within the ingroup. Like the CIA and for the same reasons, it tries to stay out of public view.

It is not accidental that *institution* is the very worst word in its vocabulary. It intends to be committed only to *"movements* not *institutions,"*[13] and yet the history of charismatic movements surely reveals that the only long-range political effectiveness lies in the search for some sort of institutionalization. There is no vision of institutional structures embodying mission, but only the tired dichotomies of structure against mission, establishment against creativity, old against new, organization against relevance.

The Renewability of the Church

Where the underground perceives the established church as ideologically immutable, some of us see it in a rapid fruit-fly mutation. Where the underground views the church leadership as if it were tranquil and secure, some of us experience it as frightened, anxious, and deeply insecure. Where the underground describes the institutional church as blind, rigid, and unwilling to enter into dialogue, some of us see the institutional church as literally thirsting for new options and models for self-understanding.

One pop necro-ecclesiologist recently wrote: "Shall we mourn the last years of a church which looks out on the world with the eyes of a federal reserve bank, staffed by uniformed guards who suspiciously peer at humanity from the safety of stained glass that is bullet-proof, fool-proof, and compassion-proof?"[14] Since reading that I have been looking around in vain for some ecclesiastical executive who feels this sense of federal reserve security in his institutional environment. Rather, quite the opposite, the actual feeling of those who have some guardian responsibility for the emerging Christian tradition is only the most acute sense of insecurity about the faltering institutional systems of our fathers' generation. Bullet-proof churches went out of style with Martin Luther King, Jr.

"There is considerably more freedom in today's institutional church to experiment with new models and images of mission than many ministers and congregations have thus far been willing to face," writes experimentalist William A. Holmes. "The slightest setback or controversy over such experiments have often caused us either to retreat to the safety of the same old patterns or to precipitously conclude that existing structures simply cannot be renewed."[15]

Total cynicism about the inertia of the establishment fails to recognize its vulnerability. Statements such as Michael Novak's might have been appropriate a decade ago, but they are not in touch with the current situation of the institutional church. Novak says, "To attempt to stand as a loyal opposition within the present establishment is, moreover, to stand on fragile and untenable ground; the inertia of the establishment is too deeply fixed for anyone to moderate its course from within."[16]

Yet, this ill-timed miscalculation is widely perpetrated among the renewing church's most creative innovators: "I am convinced that the institutional structures that we know are not renewable," says Gordon Cosby. "When the structures get as rigid and as resistant to change as they are now, perhaps the wisest strategy is not to try to renew them."[17] Again, "they hinder the proclamation of the Gospel rather than furthering it."[18]

The mutating church is searching for some option beyond the two objectionable alternatives of (*a*) totally rejecting or (*b*) simplistically defending the present institutional structures. This "third alternative" is stated by William Holmes in this way: "Some of us may simply have to be 'in process' of deciding whether the church, at this point in history, can or cannot be renewed *within* its present structures. The imperative of this position would call for laity and clergy to expend themselves on behalf of existing structures until the structures have been brought to *life* or *death*—and then give thanks to God either way they go." Holmes presses a startling analogy, which grants more to necro-ecclesiology than I would wish, but which nonetheless points to a profound theological insight: "Our role today may be that of watchfulness and keeping vigil over a body—the present institutional church—until we've seen that body buried or revived. In either case we can receive its fate of life or death from the hands of the One who gives and takes away and gives again—and has never been without some earthly vessel for the lodging of his word in Jesus Christ."[19]

THE JARGON OF RENEWAL

Two phrases in particular capture both the predicament and the promise of the renewing church: "Go where the action is" and "Let the world set the agenda." Though well intentioned, they can lead to regrettable distortions.

The church is being called to know where the action is and be there. The assumption is that God is moving in history far ahead of the church. The church must go to that arena in which God's reconciling action is most fully present in the world. Given that interpretation, the phrase has urgent significance for the life of the church today.

A more common misinterpretation turns out to be: Go where the mass media say the action is. In the past decade, the electronic media may have become the hidden tyrants of Christian social action. The slogan tends to lead one into assuming that God's action is exclusively present in some "live" areas and not present in many (perhaps most) others. Often it is assumed by some activists that the only place the church can be relevant is on the growing edge of public policy making. The negative implication: There are many areas where the action is *not!* But it is just where the grind is continuing, precisely in the midst of the ordinary, that God addresses man, and the Christian community sees the extraordinary occurring. It is precisely in these continuing structures of life that do not change in crisis or that sustain life between crises, that the Christian community also perceives the providence of God. To imply that there are some places where the action is not, is a denial of the Christian understanding of creation, where God's activity is known to be present in the totality and not merely in the special events that seem to capture the situational essence of social change.

The other phrase, which is a great deal more horrifying if used unreflectively, is the ambiguous idea of "letting the world set the agenda." Again the intention of that phrase is commendable: The world is the arena of the redemptive action of God; what is occurring in that world is very important for the church to understand and respond to if it is to be in relevant mission. To let the world set the agenda means, in its best theological sense, to let God's action in the world set the pace and the pattern for the church's action in the world.

The problem is that it often is not so understood. It is sometimes used in an uncritical sense to imply nothing less than simple, naïve, accommodation of the social environment: Let the church follow wherever the society happens to be moving; let the church become secularized in the diluted sense; let it go along with the herd, wherever it happens to be wandering or stampeding at the moment in a conformist society.

The German Christian movement is perhaps the most frightening prototype of the idea of letting the world set the agenda. The German Christians essentially held that the Nazi movement was a messianic movement, a great delivering event, the ultimate political hope of the German people. They let Hitler set the agenda. Why could not similar monstrosities appear in the current situation? It was precisely against those who were willing to say, "Let the world set the agenda" that Bonhoeffer, and many others in the German Church struggle, ultimately gave their lives. Yet simplistic phrases such as this have been the stock in trade of underground polemics.

CHAPTER 6

Toward a Conserving Radicalism

Political and religious messianists who persistently think of themselves (and not the wisdom of the body politic) as deliverers often arrogate their own theoretical "solutions" to the level of omnicompetence. Amid all their scorching criticism of all known and existing arrangements, they have a common occupational disease: a noxious lack of self-criticism.

Revolution can easily become a chameleon word bearing totally opposite meanings to different people. To some it means a familiar nineteenth-century hope for evolutionary progress, while to others it has a simple Marxian definition. Yet precisely *how* one defines revolution makes all the difference.

What we sadly lack is a theology of social change that might realistically assess the self-assertive and demonic features of our quests for messianic power, yet without cutting the nerve and vitality of constructive political change.[1] This rich combination we have seldom seen in Christian theology since the early days of Reinhold Niebuhr.

I will never forget an abrasive dialogue with a young "revolutionary" Christian from Latin America, whom I pressed on the issue of violent revolution as well as his presuppositions on Christology and ecclesiology, etc. It became quite clear that the best way historically to describe this individual was as a pietistic Christian who had simply appended to his pietism a Marxist theory of social change. One might call it pietistic Marxism. When I drove him to his religious depth, I found only the standard clichés of pietism: a weak functional Christology, a voluntaristic ecclesiology, a moralistic conception of the human predicament and the gospel, etc. To this familiar set of categories he appended a Marxian theory of revolutionary social change. It is not accidental that these two traditions of true believers find each other compatible. It is only surprising that they should think of themselves as startlingly new or original solutions.

Ten years ago if anyone had suggested that social theorists like Hegel and Hobbes would have special relevance for the 1970's, we would have responded with incredulity. Yet today we find ourselves surprised that these two thinkers, who have been written off as passé apologists for fossilized social orders, recently have become decisive in our attempts to make sense out of the contemporary crisis. Only the tragic politics of the last decade has driven us back to Hegel's dialectic and made it recognizable as a working tool. Hegel, more than any other social philosopher, may help us to grasp the multiple legitimate functions of various opposing elements in the process of revolutionary social change.

THE LOGIC OF HISTORY

From one point of view, Hegel was a great conservative social theorist. He is the hymnist of the rationality of institutional history. The rational is the real. Reason actualizes itself in institutional forms. The moral claim upon the individual is to allow himself to be shaped by the collective wisdom of human reasoning that embodies itself in institutional patterns. From one point of view he is vulnerable to being easily dismissed as a conformist, a nationalist, a social conservative who beheld in the shaping of institutions the awesome power of absolute rationality.[2]

Yet at the same time it is curious that Hegel's dialectical logic spawned the most revolutionary strategy of social change ever envisioned by man, viz., the Marxian dialectic of class struggle.[3] It is a bit difficult to discern just how Hegel's thought both applauded the continuities of history and at the same time affirmed the revolutionary challenges as functional participants in constructive social change and considered conflict to be an essential aspect of historical process. A firm grasp of his historical logic can help us today to unravel the curious interaction between revolution and conservation, between tradition and renewal, between change and continuity.[4] His dialectic simultaneously makes more sense out of both our imperatives for radical change and our cautious, deliberate, self-critical hesitations about the perils of revolution.

Not since the Civil War has our society been so torn asunder by such a total polarization of social strategies. Each polarity understands itself as the authentic bearer of the American tradition. These conflicts are dramatized daily in the clash of viewpoints between the Stroms and the Stokelys, the Agnews and the militants, the Pentagon and the selective pacifists. The centrist consensus has been exploded, perhaps irreparably, into angry polarization. The Vietnam fiasco and the urban crisis have shattered the consensus in a million directions, just as the "death of God" and "death of the church" movements shattered the ecumenical consensus in theology.

Until recently I have shared the feeling of despair about this polarized situation of estrangement. I, who have been committed to working in many situations within the liberal consensus, do not now weep for it anymore. Hegel, more than any other thinker, has helped

me to see that there are various stages or moments in the
dialectical process in which it is not only hopeful, but in
fact necessary and the only fruitful possibility, for the
consensus to dissolve, and for a revolutionary challenge
to come to awaken the central mass of society from its
slumbers to new configurations of response. The revolutionary has a significant role to play at a certain nexus
of history, when a whole set of presuppositions needs to
be radically challenged, even though the revolutionary
himself may be entrapped in all sorts of illusory assumptions and may not be able in any sense to pull off the
brand of social change he envisions as desirable.[5]

Hegel's theory of tragedy throws special light upon
these seemingly tragic circumstances. The key element of
tragedy is contradiction, the opposition of one moral
claim or value against another. The essence of tragedy
lies "in a conflict between spiritual forces which belong
to one system and which ought to be in harmony. The
catastrophe is the assertion by the whole of its complexity
against the one-sidedness of some imperfect aspect. When
the conflict is between two individuals, each, from the
tragic point of view, is dominated by some aspect of the
whole good . . . followed to the exclusion of all else. The
devotion to this abstract ideal, good in itself but imperfect when set against the rest of life, brings the agent
into collision with the other factors and with the whole;
and in the conflict the tragic hero is overthrown. The
final note of tragedy, however, is not loss. Behind the
sympathy with the fallen there must be a feeling of the
greater good which the agent himself was unable to
grasp, and his fall is a vindication of the deeper truth."[6]

Revolutionary political positions are in this same way
kairotically functional.[7] At a particular moment of history they may function meaningfully even though they
do not represent an enduring or adequate philosophy of
social change.[8] This is how we may come to celebrate the

very polarization so painfully present in current political life.

Hegel more than any other philosopher of history can help us to think dialectically about this process, and in a sense to share imaginatively and sympathetically in the whole dialectic, not standing partisanly in one point only of the dialectic, nor standing apart as an abstract non-participant, but to see the dialectic at work and to understand its various moments of thesis and antithesis as valid and necessary toward the whole process. I myself hunger to embrace the whole process as a conserving radical, conserving the basis of revolutionary action, seeking to transform the present as rapidly and realistically as possible, without the loss of the best resources of the historic tradition. What is finally important is not one single moment of that process, but the process itself, which is another way of talking about the Lordship, presence, and revelation of God in history (cf. Pannenberg).[9]

Far from being sheer romanticism or reaction, Hegel's thought was in its historical context a profound source of renewal.[10] It was capable of affirming the destruction of dysfunctional institutions, as well as the emerging challenges in history, but it was more so a celebration of the reestablishment of equilibrium in history through a constant process of conflict and reconciliation. This kind of thinking can provide us an urgently needed perspective amid the destruction of past orders in which most of us have certain emotional investments. It can also free us to be more critical toward the pretensions toward total discontinuity in the revolutionary mentality.[11]

In this frame of reference, no proposition can be simply true or false, when considered abstractly apart from its historical context. The truth occurs in history. In a sense the truth is history occurring. Therefore when we stand within one narrow nexus of history and audaciously attempt to judge a particular aspect as true or false, we tend easily to abstract ourselves out of the truth, which is the whole concrete historical process occurring. The Hegelian pattern affirms the relativism of various historical options and yet sees in each of them some expression of the absolute, i.e., of reason working itself out in history. Each new stage expresses the whole force of the absolute at that particular point in time, even though it may be a very limited and transitory position if seen within the whole.[12]

The driving force of the dialectic is contradiction. Conflict is creative. If there were no revolutionary challenges to the *status quo,* then there would be no social change, no history, no organic growth of humanity in time. Every change is both continuous and discontinuous. Both the continuities and discontinuities are meaningful.[13]

A CONSERVING RADICALISM

The deepest radicalism is the radicalism that is already incipient in the Western intellectual tradition, particularly in the Judeo-Christian hope. The most radical statement in church and society today is a more profound conservatism which seeks the renewal of that tradition.

Conversely, it is impossible to be an authentic conserver of the best traditions of human wisdom without at the same time being something of a radical. One cannot renew traditional wisdom unless one is willing to wake up to the revolutionary character of history. To be an authentic conserver today, one must allow the contemporary world clearly to address the tradition with its own questions, concerns, despairs, and hopes.

The blacks are achieving a new sense of self-identity precisely *through* a study of their history. This is what contemporary ahistorical Christianity must do. Like the black community, it must rediscover itself through serious reflection on its own actual rootage, not just its imagined or ideologically conceived past. It is not a matter of mythmaking. Black studies at its best is not a process of picking out what sounds good and flattering the black man with an idealized past. It is rather looking at the historical process itself, letting it speak honestly to the present. Similarly the Christian community will get its bearings only through a thoroughly honest dialogue with its past. We must address that history with our own postmodern questions, and we must allow that history to address us with its questions.

The conserving mentality most worth listening to is that which listens with all its might to the human past so that its historic resources can impinge now upon the shaping of the future. The only genuine conservatism in a revolutionary context is that which presses its own conserving character self-critically to its depth. A shallow, historically ignorant, defensive, or merely tactical conservatism is no longer plausible. Only the conserver who asks how the tradition can be relevantly renewed is faithful to the tradition.

CHAPTER 7

The Strange Case of the Invisible Church

Whatever might have been the intent of classical theories of the invisibility of the church, it is clear that they did not intend to imply that the church as an embodied community would cease to exist, or that it should become totally absorbed in the world so as to lose its own distinctive identity. Rather, quite the opposite. *A principal function of the notion of the invisible church in the history of Christian doctrine has been to refocus and thereby validate the mission of the visible church.* The whole notion of the invisible church is only conceivable in relation to a visible church. The invisible church was never properly asserted in such a way as to deny wholly the visible church. Until recently this idea has never functioned as a desperate flight from embarrassing bodily, visible, institutional forms.

Some subterraneans carry on a vigorous polemic against the visible, institutional church, explicitly or implicitly assuming that they themselves constitute the "true church." Appeals continue to be made to the concept of an "invisible" church. This notion of *ecclesia invisibilis* has enjoyed a long and dubious history. In order to assess these appeals more circumspectly, we propose to make a careful review of this notion in its basic phases of development. Although it may seem like an unnecessarily lengthy detour, this historical exercise will help us get our bearings in dealing with the current underground.

It was Ignatius who taught that just as the incarnation is the union of the seen with the unseen, of God with man, so the church is at the same time a union of the invisible with the visible, of spirit with flesh.[1] As early as the first century the church thought of itself as the *body* of Christ, forming a spiritual union with him, as mysterious as the incarnation itself. When the early church fathers spoke of the mystery of *corpus Christi,* they were clearly assuming an empirical and visible community. There was not yet any hint of an "invisible" church that could be abstracted or divorced from the visible church.

One of the earliest challenges to the notion of the visible church came from the Gnostics, who conceived the church in such highly mystical terms that it tended to become dehistorized and totally spiritualized.[2] It was in an attempt to counteract this dehistorizing tendency that Irenaeus began to argue that in the church there is one faith, which can be seen throughout the whole known world, one doctrine, and an unbroken succession of bishops, which links the visible church with the apostles, the continuity of which guarantees the unity and authenticity of the church's faith.[3]

It was in the revolt of Montanism that the notion of the church as a strictly charismatic society developed. The Montanists viewed the reality of the church not as a visible, organizational body, but as an invisible, spiritualist movement. In fact, many of the Montanists were so determined to make sure that there were no sinners in the church, that they proceeded to "purify" the church, to excommunicate and expunge from the church all elements of sin. It was against that fanatical ecclesiology that the ecumenical church, led by Callistus, the bishop of Rome, argued that according to the parable of the tares, sinners should be permitted to remain in the church.[4]

Origen proposed that the body of Christ is not merely the church, but the whole of humanity, since ultimately all of humanity and all of creation will be brought into the reconciling reality of God's love. If all humanity is to be saved ultimately, all men must in some sense belong to the church, even though they may not participate *de facto* in its visible forms.[5]

It was Cyprian, whose views became familiar to all subsequent Western fathers, who said: "He cannot have God for his father who has not the church for his mother," and "There is no salvation outside the church" (*salus extra ecclesiam non est*). In this period the episcopacy became viewed as the essence of the church and as that which guarantees the unity of the church.[6]

While Alexandrian spirituality tended to dehistoricize the church, stressing its essence as spiritual, while deemphasizing its organizational, hierarchical aspects, Rome tended to identify the true church with its institutional embodiment. Just how that balance between spirit and structure can be worked out has been *the* problem of ecclesiology for twenty centuries, and it remains our essential predicament today.

The idea of the invisible church, however, received decisive shape with Augustine in connection with the Donatist controversy. It was commonly held among patristic theologians at this time (notably Hilary) that the church was a mixed society (*corpus permixtum*) which included some unworthy of the name Christian. During the Donatist controversy certain North African bishops were accused by the Donatists of unfaithful acts (specifically, they surrendered copies of the Scriptures to civil authorities during the persecution of Diocletian in A.D. 303). The Donatists, with a purist conception of the church as a *de facto* holy body, insisted that these allegedly disloyal bishops should not be followed. They claimed that the validity of the Sacraments depended upon the worthiness of the minister and that the church ceased to be holy when it tolerated unworthy leaders.[7]

A decisive moment in ecclesiological history came when Augustine responded to the Donatists throughout a long period of controversy. Much that Augustine taught was in accord with previous ecclesiology: no salvation apart from the church; the church is the body of Christ; the one holy catholic church is associated with the church of Rome and its sacramental life; the church is composed of both the wheat and the tares, a *corpus permixtum* of good and evil.[8] It was Augustine, however, who first began to draw a deliberate and fateful distinction between the invisible and visible church, i.e., between an essential church which is composed of those who are in Christ in faith, hope, and love, as distinguished, but not separated, from an outward, visible, empirical church.

The Donatists had forced the issue: How can the church be holy if it embraces sinners? Augustine answered with a very significant concession: Only the elect are, in the proper sense, Christ's body. Sinners who (although baptized and recipients of the Sacraments) are not living in faith, hope, and love may seem to be within the church, but they are not a part of the *invisibilis caritatis compages*.[9] Sinners and hypocrites may be found inside the house, but remain alien to its inward life.

It was strictly on the basis of this hypothesized invisible church that Augustine argued that "in God's ineffable foreknowledge many who seem to be without are within, and many who seem to be within are without."[10] For the most part, however, it is clear that Augustine assumed that the invisible church is present somewhere *within* the boundaries of the holy, Roman Catholic Church.[11]

The Roman bishops emphasized the unity and catholicity of the church while less stress was put on its holiness. The Donatists upheld a certain understanding of holiness at the price of the dissolution of the unity and catholicity of the church. In my view, the concept of the holiness of the church held by both the Donatists and Augustine led to a serious misconception of the nature of the church, since the most profound holiness of the church is its willingness to receive forgiveness of sin Therefore both the Donatists' proto-puritanism and Augustine's response to it placed the doctrine of the visible church in a fate-laden framework from which it still suffers today.

It should be remembered, however, that Augustine was thinking out of a rich Platonic tradition in which there was a profound realism about the invisible which we can no longer assume on the basis of naturalistic empiricism. To suggest that something was invisible, according to Augustine, was not to imply that it was any less experienceable or real or related to history. As a matter of fact, it was quite the opposite. In the Platonic understanding, the most real is the most invisible, whereas the embodiment of any idea is always less than the idea itself. In contrast to the Platonic tendency, the Hebraic understanding of the people of God clearly had a more visible, concrete, and historical character. To the extent to which Augustine borrowed from his neo-Platonic environment, he tended toward a dilution of the Hebraic conception of community, which always presupposed actual human beings and nations and visible social structures. Of course, Augustine did not ever deny the visibility of the church. But in his assertion of the invisibility of the true church, he tended to leave the unstated implication to some of those who later interpreted him that the invisible church is not only distinguishable, but separable from the visible church.

Eastern Christianity in the medieval period put less

stress upon the organizational, legal, institutional aspects of the church than occurred in the West. Rather, Eastern ecclesiology was focused on communion with the incarnate Savior and the mystery of the liturgy. The roots of Eastern ecclesiology are in the Athanasian dictum: "Christ became man that we might become divine."[12] Upon this Christology, Eastern Christianity began to build its understanding of the church as the mystical body for preserving, transmitting, and celebrating the mystery of God's saving action in Christ.[13]

In Western tradition, however, considerably more stress was placed upon the visible continuity of the church, its hierarchical solidification, and much controversy focused on the issue of Roman supremacy. Visibility was a powerful theme of medieval piety, as may be seen in its art and architecture, adoration of relics, and above all in its sacramental thought.

Among proto-protestant expressions of the notion of invisibility, none is more impressive than John Wycliffe's view of the church as the "totality of the predestinated." Attributing infallibility only to the Scriptures, Wycliffe denied the papacy and episcopal continuity. He protested the pretense that the church is synonymous with an objective and existing body of visible persons. The predestined are invisibly scattered in the midst of the world, visible only to God.

In *De dominio divino* and *De civili dominio*, Wycliffe argued that dominion, or power, is a gift of grace, and that since the present state of the visible church is so corrupt as to preclude any true *dominio* or lordship, it is appropriate that governments confiscate ecclesiastical property.[14] Like many today, Wycliffe thought the church could be improved only by being deprived of its worldly riches.

Thomas Aquinas stressed the oneness and the sociality of the church. He regarded schism as inimical to the church's nature. He strongly emphasized the one body analogy: "The entire church is called a single mystical body, by analogy with the physical body, which performs different functions through different members. . . . Looking at the whole course of history, then, we say that Christ is the Head of all mankind, but not of all men in the same way. First and principally, of those who are united to him in glory; secondly, of those who are actually united with him by charity; thirdly, of those actually united to him by faith; fourthly, of those not yet united actually but who are predestined to heaven; fifthly, of those who could be united but will not be—these are human beings living in the world who are not predestined, and who will, on their passing away, wholly cease to be members of Christ, even potentially."[15]

The question of the church's visibility or invisibility was hotly contested during the Reformation period and in part was a restatement of Augustinian issues. It has often been charged that the Reformation's uncertainty about this question opened the door for division in the church, since many separate societies came to bear the name of the authentic church. The belief that the true church is invisibly one did, in one sense, help to maintain the notion of the unity of the church despite its historical fragmentations. But it is ironic that the notion of the invisible unity of the church was precisely the basis upon which the actual schisms in the church emerged. Bellarmine was among those who early recognized this irony.

Luther shared many of the tendencies we have already observed in the Eastern fathers: a strong emphasis upon the spirituality of the church and a corresponding suspicion of outward forms. According to Luther, the church consists of "those who rely on nothing else than God's grace and mercy."[16] In characteristically earthy language, Luther developed this startling analogy on sinners in the church: "To be sure they are members of the church, as much as spit, snot, pus, sweat, feces, urine, scabs, smallpox, ulcers, syphilis, and all contagious diseases are members of the body. These are things also in and on the body. Yea, as blotches and filth which the body must bear with great danger, pains, and disgust."[17]

Luther applied the distinction between seeing and believing to the visible and invisible church in a fateful way: he associated *seeing* with the visible church and with the whole Roman apologia for the church, whereas in *believing* one participates in the true church by faith. Does this suggest an indirect polemic against the visibility of the church? It is true that Luther did strongly emphasize the primacy of believing over against seeing, but nonetheless the *communio sanctorum* was always assumed by Luther to be a visible body, though its deeper reality could not be established on an outward or structural basis. Luther argued wisely that *the authentic church is only visible to the community of faith.* It is not visible to disbelief, or to man's natural, corrupt reason. "Of these matters the flesh is not able to see or judge anything."[18] Despite the institutionalizing tendency of later Lutheranism, there is a fair dose of spiritualistic ecclesiology in Luther himself, who said, "The true, real, right, essential church is a matter of the spirit and not of anything external."[19]

Luther himself was caught in the same dilemma we have witnessed in the Augustinian-Donatist controversy. He was in dialogue with Rome on the one hand, the left wing of the Reformation on the other. Whereas Rome tended to assert the quasi-identity of the visible church with the true church, Luther had to assert faith in Word and Sacrament as the essential definition of the church. But on the other hand, there were certain left-wing spiritualists who believed the church needed no structure at all, but only individual charisma or contemplation.

Against them Luther asserted that without Word and Sacrament there is no church.

Melanchthon, however, differed from Luther's latitudinarianism. Especially in his later teachings, Melanchthon stressed the notion that the church is a visible organization in which the pure word is preached, pure doctrine taught, and the Sacraments properly administered.[20] Struggling against the spiritualistic left wing, Melanchthon was afraid of the tendency toward anti-institutional fanaticism, iconoclasm, and chiliasm. So with Melanchthon the institutional and visible character of the church was again reasserted.

In the theology of Calvin, the church, as the community of the elect is, as in Wycliffe, invisible, and known finally only to God. The elect are found in an empirical, visible structure, which has as its marks Word, Sacrament, and works of love.[21] Although the faithful know of the invisible church by faith, they also respect and cultivate the visible church, which also includes hypocrites and sinners. Calvin strongly emphasized, as did the early Catholic sources, that severance from the church is a denial of God's providence. "Calvin always antagonized with the greatest energy the conclusion which sectarian leaders might deduce from his premises, that the external organization of the church is of small importance. He emphasized the necessity of ecclesiastical forms and ordinances more strongly than Melanchthon himself."[22]

Although the elect are not visible to natural perception, nonetheless wherever the signs of the visible church (confession of faith, participation in the Sacraments, and the disciplined life) are present, one may be sure that the Spirit is at work calling the church into being. Despite Calvin's vigorous advocacy of invisibility, there was no thought that the invisible church was a denial or abrogation of its visibility. Even though the church in some ways may be impure (even "in ruins"), and even though the marks are not fully present, Calvin still did not deny the title of church to the corrupted church.[23]

Calvin called his major theological treatise, not incidentally, *The Institutes.* Calvin was followed by a creative Reformed tradition which was concerned in an unparalleled way with visible institution-building, both in church and society.[24]

Anglican ecclesiology took a *via media* between Geneva and Rome. "The church," according to Richard Hooker, "is always a visible society of men."[25] It may be a mixed society of sinners and faithful, but there is no doubt of its visibility. Cranmer and Hooker used the term "invisible church" as a synonym for the mystical body of Christ. "The visible church may include some who do not truly belong to the invisible, or the church invisible contain some not apparently numbered in the visible church, but normally it is expected that members of the visible church belong to the invisible. One cannot be called the true church and the other the false."[26]

It was the Roman Catholic controversialist Robert Bellarmine who in *De ecclesia militante* lashed out at the Protestant tendency to imagine the true church as invisible, to overemphasize the subjective elements, and not to give enough emphasis to the external, objective reality of the church. Against the illusion of a pure church, he argued with good precedent that the believer or catechumen first must place himself in the context of the church where grace can grow. It is not necessary first to perfect some internal grace before one participates in the church. It is precisely the external church through its Sacraments which nourishes that grace. In order to be a member of the church one only needs to profess faith externally and participate in the Sacraments. From that point, sacramental grace nurtures the Christian life.[27]

Among sixteenth-century Scottish divines the invisible-visible distinction became further defined: "The Scottish Reformers appear to have thought (a) that the Church is necessarily embodied, (b) that the embodiment is always a good in itself, (c) that the embodiment is nevertheless liable to disease, and (d) that the radical surgery the cure may entail is the work of Christ, the Head, by the Holy Spirit working through the ministry. The 'Kirk Malignant' is not really another Church at all, for the Church is one; it is, rather, a parasite on the True Church. It could not live by itself, for it is its life to feed upon the Church it seeks to devour."[28] All this, according to Geddes MacGregor, was consonant with Calvin's ecclesiology.

"What is visibly presented," concludes MacGregor, "is the divine activity operating in and through the Church, human sin and folly notwithstanding. The manifestation of human sin and folly that most conspicuously obscures the visibility of the Church's wholeness is our failure as members of the Body of Christ to yield ourselves entire, body and soul, to the *koinonia* of the Body. . . . So what appears as the fragmentariness of the visible Church is but the shadow of the fragmentariness of the participation of ourselves in the life of the Body. It is not to be expected that, being ourselves imperfectly willing to realize our ingrafting into the Body, we shall be able to see more than an imperfect visible expression of the principle of unity of that Body in whose life we inadequately participate."[29]

Due to their persistent stress upon the fallenness of the visible church in the post-Constantinian era, the Anabaptists have often been accused of developing an esoteric, invisible conception of the church.[30] Recent studies, however, are showing that the charge is regrettably overstated. Although the early Anabaptists did often protest the Constantinian fall of the church and its subsequent alliance with the world, nevertheless whenever they began to speak about the restitution of the church, they always were referring to a thoroughly visible community.[31]

Significantly enough, the Anabaptists acknowledged that their own teaching on the church was unimportant apart from their attempt to give it actual embodiment in living social organisms. The terrible history of their persecution shows their determination to manifest their faith by the creation of visible Christian communities. The marks of the true church, accordingly, were: believer's baptism, spiritual government, the Lord's Supper, and the life of *koinonia,* all of which not only can but must be visibly embodied.[32]

This is as far as we can go in this short historical review of the notion of *ecclesia invisibilis.* We can only briefly mention two other movements that influenced the doctrine of the church in subsequent periods—pietism and rationalism. Under the influence of such leaders as Spener and Wesley, pietism reconceived the visibility of the church in terms of the small, committed community of believers whose lives had been reshaped by the power of the Holy Spirit. In pietism the notion of *ecclesiolae in ecclesia* (churches within the church) enabled the converted communities to think of themselves as leaven within the larger *corpus permixtum.*

Under the influence of rationalism, the visible church was understood mainly as the community where the truth is being sought. The sacerdotal and institutional functions tended to become vestigial. Liberal Protestantism later absorbed the pietistic emphasis on the personal with the rationalistic emphasis on reason, welcoming into the church the powerful ideological and intellectual developments of the nineteenth century: historicism, philosophical idealism, and various views of social change.

Why have we delved into this long and complex history of the *ecclesia invisibilis?* Because veiled appeals are so often made both by reformers and the establishment to this elusive concept. It deserves to be clarified in the light of its long and complex history.

In its principal forms the doctrine of invisibility has served certain useful functions in the history of theology: (1) It has deprived the church of the pride by which it would arrogate to itself finality, or presume that its institutional boundaries were essentially synonymous with the true church. (2) It has provided a way to conceive of the unity of the church precisely amid its seeming historical fragmentation. (3) It has often functioned as a vital means of reformation and critique of corruption in the visible church.

On the other hand, the problems and inconsistencies of the doctrine are persistent and troublesome: (1) The notion of invisibility has sometimes been employed in such a way as to deny or neglect the essential visibility and historicity of the church. (2) It can easily turn into a simplistic and even cynical rejection of all institutional forms, imagining that the farther one gets from organizational structure, the closer one comes to the reality of the church. (3) Despite vague appeals to the invisible unity of the true church, actually it may become a divisive cause of schism, even in the name of ecumenicity. (4) The doctrine of invisibility still tends toward an excessively puritanical conception of the church as a holy or perfected body. It fails to acknowledge the sinfulness of the church. It is willing to embrace the church only in purist forms. Thus it is persistently frustrated with everything that it sees happening in the church, which is composed of visible, imperfect structures and ordinary people who always in some way calculate their own interests into their participation in the *communio sanctorum*.

Is the concept of invisibility useful today? From its

history we can see that it has often functioned as a meaningful critique of corruption in the visible church, and we might expect it to continue to function in that way. But it is also clear from this history that it lends itself easily to misinterpretation, abstraction, and romanticism which easily turns into divisiveness and fragmentation.

Part III

THE HIDDEN OPPORTUNITY

CHAPTER 8

The Revolutionary Now

EXISTENCE AS REVOLUTION

We all experience the pervasive, compelling power of change in our time. Change *is* our time. Modernity consists of the process of death and new creation.

From the beginning of man's toilsome movement through history, this is the hidden pattern of the mosaic: death and renewal. In some moments of historical crisis, such as ours, the pace quickens, corners are turned more rapidly, revolution is in the wind. Yet in all times of man's story it has been the same, if sameness means change. He has had to face the reality of time, which means birth, risk, growth, decision, commitment, process, deterioration, senility, death, new birth—in short, temporal existence.

Frail words only glimpse, barely touch the reality to which we are trying to point, which is revolution, which is our times, which is human history. It is difficult to bring this thought into full consciousness, to hold it up for lucid awareness, since we train ourselves so deliberately not to see it. So much do we hunger for security and rootage in time that we desperately seek to protect ourselves even against the recognizing of the awesome reality in which we stand. But time is there, always quietly or abrasively calling us to ourselves as temporal beings.

Let us put the point in a single, direct image: We resemble dinosaurs. Everyone born of nineteenth-century Christian individualism has some dinosaur bones in his body. We are the last generation that will ever live in the world we have known, with our ideologies, our hang-ups, our presuppositions. Most of us have enjoyed being dinosaurs—those giant, marvelous beasts roaming the earth. But some new, lesser, punier but craftier species are emerging that bite at our vulnerabilities, attack us while we are not watching. It all seems so unfair, but it is happening.

The dinosaur is an image of extinction. It reminds us of the total demise of a remarkable species, one of the greatest that has ever imprinted the earth. This is how many of us now experience the liberal Christian tradition —a great tradition, not to be ridiculed just because it is now vulnerable. It is magnificent; it has had a great history, but is now extremely vulnerable.

The dinosaur was vulnerable precisely because it did not prove capable of sufficiently relevant and rapid mutation. When the ice patterns and glacial flows and swamplands changed, the species was not capable of adjusting itself to the new historical conditions, and did not produce mutants which could adjust, whereas the smaller, less impressive beasts did mutate, or their previous mutations enabled them to meet the new environment.

Ours is no abstract or archaic question. You and I are bound up in a history that is exploding with revolutionary change. We are enmeshed in institutional structures in which we have invested much of ourselves, structures that are in radical confusion and transition. We experience profound anxieties about these social structures. We are bound up in our institutional environments, and whether we like them or not, when we speak of changing our institutions we are speaking of changing ourselves. We are not involved in an esoteric discussion the result of which makes no difference, but rather we are discussing our future, or even more decisively our possibility for having a future.

Since the mission of the church is in and for the world, it is called to negotiate history ever anew. New gifts are constantly being borne to it by the giver of history, however often it may be that the church refuses to behold these gifts. Certain senile structures are constantly in the process of being judged inadequate by history, no matter how closely the church might have bound itself to those forms.[1]

Facing historical risk is nothing new for the Christian community.[2] It had been in existence for only a few decades when it had to face the fall of Jerusalem and the consequent diaspora of the Jewish civilization by which it had been spawned. It was less than a century old when it began to face severe persecution from the most powerful military apparatus in the ancient world. It was only four centuries old when, after having just learned finally to trust in the Roman political order, that state collapsed and it had to make another radical adjustment. If the church had not been reshaped by men of immense historical imagination, it might never have negotiated those dangerous crises so as to become the predominating force in Western culture for the next thousand years.

As always, the now world confronts a coming world. Certain modes of culture, styles of life, are now emergent. In amazement, we behold their birth and promise. Familiar patterns of culture are visibly dying. Death and birth: that is what history is about. There is no finite reality, no creaturely object, no human good, no contextual value, no living process which is not subject to this flux and risk. These are the elements of history, the components of life itself.

The eucharistic community, the mutating church, embraces and affirms this entire process in a special way. Without spelling out an entire theology from creation to consummation, we can at least clarify what goes on concretely in Christian worship. Essentially, the eucharistic community celebrates the giver of this change and very process of emergence. Christian faith gives thanks to the One who enables new possibilities to emerge in history. It rejoices in the newness of each morning, each new dawn of historical occurrence, each and every birth of every new creature. It gives thanks for the One who is constantly presenting new possibilities for self-actualization.

But what about death? Is death affirmable in the same way? That is a tougher, but equally decisive, question. For we ourselves are threatened by anxiety and death. We know that we are vulnerable, finite, and we die. Yet the Judeo-Christian memory, when it is being true to itself, confronts the deteriorations of history, the senilities and deaths, with an equally resounding affirmation: the One who meets us as the source of all good is also the same One who meets us at the end of our human achievements.

In this temporal order, we are constantly faced with the fact that the good things we enjoy are vulnerable to frustration, erosion by time, and finally to death. No matter how much I love my children, they may reject me, or be taken away from me by war or sickness or intergenerational conflict. If I idolatrize my cherished relationships, I may have to face the fact that my gods are subject to death. These finite relationships are all limited. The boundary? Jews and Christians address that boundary as Father! Lord! Deliverer! The Judeo-Christian community stands, remarkably enough, in the midst of this historical process and says, "Though he slay me, yet will I trust in him."[3] This community has from time to time learned to receive both the process of creativity and the process of dissolution as the gift of the One who gives us life, the same eternal reality who has made known his care and love for all humanity.

THE BONDAGE TO SENILITY

Our next thesis: The church, throughout its entire history, has had a persistent tendency to get itself indebted to deteriorating cultural forms. It has been constantly tempted to rigidify alliances with passing, not emerging, political and cultural patterns, which are either dying or in fact often quite dead. Like Houdini locking himself in a trunk to be thrown into a raging river, the church has seemed bent on locking itself into certain senile cultural patterns and then playing a breathless game with history to see if at the last minute, just before its dying gasp, it can escape. Its indebtedness to feudal society or to hereditary monarchies, e.g., made it extremely difficult for many parts of the church to enter into a realistic relationship with the developing world of capitalistic economy or democratic political processes.

Why is this? Why does the church get itself so hopelessly enmeshed in social structures that have long outlived their usefulness? Because the Christian ethic and mentality has had a pastoral, caring relation to cultural situations and social structures. It is led by its empathetic participation in various social structures to value those structures highly. That is not necessarily bad. We are not proposing that the church remain aloof from realistic involvement in political, economic, and familial structures. But when specific historical patterns become so firmly identified with the essence of the church that you cannot see the difference between Christianity and culture, a crisis in identity results which may be dangerous to the very health and continuity of the body of Christ. It must be born anew institutionally, just as it calls for rebirth personally, in order to get itself back into history.

Let us sharpen the thesis: When the church gets itself in bondage to deteriorating cultural forms, it tends to become isolated from the emerging forms.[4] To the extent that the church finds itself in bondage to senile subcultures, it finds itself alienated from emerging subcultures.

We are not suggesting, and in fact we specifically reject, the idea that futurity is by definition good, that whatever is new is good, that what is emerging is to be more highly valued than what is dying. Rather, our thesis is that when the church identifies its very being and mission with certain cultural forms, it tends to become increasingly unwilling to venture with seemingly peripheral, yet perhaps extremely promising, new forms. It is increasingly unfree to be the church, to confront the future, to celebrate the gift of the creative process with hope and care and trust. Its failure to embrace the new is a basic form of unfaithfulness.

To some generations it is given to build—to other generations is given the task of enduring the destruction of these previously developed structures. What is the task of our generation? It is much more dramatically captured by the image of a burning city than that of a perfectly or maturely constructed city. To picture our times, one must not avoid facing the reality of destruction.

What I am trying to express about revolution is rooted in my own personal history. It is me, what I experience every day. I experience something that looks like rioting, bombing, burning, and destruction every day—morally, aesthetically, institutionally, personally, sociologically, psychologically, religiously. Each day we must deal with a historical situation in which many of the institutional patterns that we had once imagined to be secure are in fact cracking up. That is an awesome awareness. We examine those cracks. They go down into the foundation.[5]

History is like this. New shapes and forms devour the old ones. New technologies, new languages, slaughter and demolish the old. That is what revolution means: destruction and renewal.

To speak of cultural destruction is not to imply an absence of creative potentiality. In fact quite the opposite, so much new is coming into being that we cannot even assimilate it into our expanding consciousness. But we whose roots are in Western history are now experiencing that some of the familiar cultural assumptions with which we have grown up may be suffering terminal illnesses. We have done the very thing against which the prophets warned: absolutized the limited, idealized the finite, made idols out of created things.

When we realize that the limited, contextual goods we have exalted to gods are in the midst of collapsing, we experience anxiety. For ours is an age in which structures and substructures are being whittled out from under us, structures that we never thought could be whittled. We feel the earth quaking beneath our feet. There is something new going on in history, something moving, bigger than the all of us. It is an unexpected earthquake. We were not prepared for this transition. We might have been prepared for the one that happened last century, but not this.

Typically and tragically, the lethargic church seems always to be preparing for revolutions that have just occurred two or three generations back. The church is now more or less ready for the great frontier experience, for those days when we were dealing with rural, individualistic, personalistic society, with one-to-one relationships abounding all around. We are now ready to embrace that world, to preach on the frontier. That is not our world. The Christian community has gotten itself again indebted to a world that is already in the process of passing away.

THE MORAL PLAUSIBILITY OF EMERGENT SUBCULTURES

A special moral perplexity of the church in our society is that it has lost its previously assured sense of moral authority among the generation that really counts, namely, the emerging generation. Who really listens to the church? Obviously not the youth, at least not much. It is only to the parent generation that the church speaks with moral credibility. When we speak of "the crisis in authority" we are speaking essentially of a crisis for the parent generation, not for the emerging generation.

In an effort to grasp this perplexity in a broader frame of reference, we propose the following hypothesis: In certain periods of history, particular subcultures or social groups assume or achieve a weightier moral plausibility than other groups, and often for very particularized and opaque historical reasons. Often this plausibility is not, strictly speaking, earned. It is given. It is simply a gift of history, or of a certain constellation of events that create a certain moment of moral plausibility for that group. Credibility thus may be viewed in relation to the Biblical understanding of providence, as a sheer "given" of history. It may be what the Christian tradition has called *charisma,* or gift, or grace.

To what subcultures can we now point who experience this "given" moral credibility? Above all, blacks and youth.

The moral judgments of blacks are listened to by both friend and foe with special care today. They have credibility. Why? What goes into this mystique of credibility? However interesting the question, it goes far beyond the scope of this inquiry. Our purpose here is not to make a value judgment about whether or not the blacks deserve moral credibility, or to analyze the anatomy of it, but rather merely to make a historical judgment that, in fact, they do have credibility.

The embarrassing corollary, of course, is that there is a serious lack of moral plausibility among whites. It is precisely because we are white Anglo-Saxons that some of us have lost our moral plausibility. It may seem totally unfair, but there are good reasons why. To many emergent peoples, the "WASP" (we may hate that designation for white-Anglo-Saxon-Protestant, but it is the very fact that the designation is hated that interests us at the moment) tradition has represented nothing but oppression, pride, slavery, dehumanization, and bitterness. Whether we like it or not, many of us are the privileged beneficiaries of this elite tradition which has in some ways been on the cutting edge of history for several centuries. We are the inheritors of it, and we inherit not only its achievements but also its cancerous sores, wounds, dilemmas, and injustices. Regardless of our good, bad, or mixed motives, depressed peoples perceive us as if our main goal were that of maintaining our power, which to them has consistently spelled oppression. Despite our fervent disclaimers, white Anglo-Saxon churchmen are perceived as legitimizers of white Anglo-Saxon power. Whatever we may say or even do about justice, peace, charity, or the brotherhood of man, all that the developing peoples often hear is our tendency to legitimize and give some sort of phony cosmic support for our particular social structures, economic ideologies, and political power bases which they experience as thoroughly demonic and horrifying.

This is why there is a plausibility gap between the traditional white man's consciousness of his own moral authority and the rising expectations of depressed peoples. Only a generation or two ago, there still remained a vast reservoir of moral authority which was ascribed to "Western Christian culture." Europeans and Americans would go to Africa or Asia assuming that their superior technologies and wealth and power would be acknowledged with awe. Not so today. We mistake the contemporary situation if we still assume we can trade on any of that moral plausibility. With Vietnam it is completely bankrupt.

Regrettably, for many of us the whole image of the church is firmly tied in with this bankruptcy. The church, as in many previous ages, has allowed itself to become deeply indebted to a particular set of obsolete social assumptions and values which in fact are in disrepute among a majority of the emerging world.

HISTORICAL PATTERNS

Our next thesis: This revolutionary context in which we are enmeshed is not structurally different from many other painful cultural crises which the church has had to negotiate in its crisis-ridden history. If we could sensitize our awareness to the risks the church has taken in the past in dealing with emergent cultures, we would not feel so hopeless about the risk we are being asked to take. The pedagogy of history will reveal analogies between our dilemma and past dilemmas through which the church has worked. Any community that has faced twenty centuries of awesome historical change has had to mutate many times.

Basic mutations have occurred in ecclesial self-understanding in at least three pivotal periods: (1) The mutation into the Hellenistic world from late Judaism, (2) the mutation into the Teutonic world, and (3) the mutation into the modern world.

The church's first mutation was demanded in its first century, as it emerged embryonically out of Judaic culture into the strange new Hellenistic world. Born amid late Judaic apocalypticism, the early church moved toward the Hellenistic world with many misgivings, and with the Hebraic ethos imprinted on its very language and thought forms. Yet it was forced to come to terms with this alien culture as it moved through Syria, Asia Minor, Greece, and the Roman world. The question: How did the primitive church negotiate this massive cultural metamorphosis? The issue focused symbolically on circumcision. Basically it was a question of whether the Christian community would remain essentially identified with Jewish cultus, or undergo some sort of unknown, risky Hellenistic mutation. Now, as we look safely back upon it, the transition may seem rather painless and natural. But if we had been required to make the hard choices faced by the early Christian missionaries, as Jews in a Greco-Roman world, surely we would have felt much of the same sense of "mission impossible" that we now feel as we face "alien" Marxist and secular cultures and new technological environments.

A second crucial mutation may be seen in the troubled transition from the Roman world into medieval society. The Constantinian church had become the established religion of the Roman Empire. But that happened just before the Roman state virtually fell to pieces with the sacking of Rome in A.D. 410. What historical power crushed the might of Rome? Surprisingly, the illiterate barbaric hordes from northern Europe, first Alaric and the Goths, and then others. By then many Christians had come to assume that the destiny of the church was tied up with the maintenance of the Roman Empire. For four centuries the church had negotiated many crises with and against Rome. By the beginning of the fifth century it was just beginning to achieve a sense of clear self-identity under the post-Constantinian rapprochement of church and state. The church had deepened its roots in the Roman tradition of law and in Greco-Roman culture.

The fall of Rome constituted a crisis in credibility in the Christian tradition. It was robbed of its newly found "place" in the world. This constituted a massive, cultural, moral, and intellectual crisis for the church, similar in scope to that which we face today with the "engulfing hordes of secularization."

The question arose as to how, amid revolutionary change, the church could mutate without losing its essential sameness, its rootage in history, its apostolicity. Nothing had seemed more secure than Rome. Now the church had to decide about its destiny in a future bereft of the Roman imperium. It was precisely amid this radical transition, when history seemed up for grabs, that Augustine wrote *De civita Dei,* providing a broad overview of the historical process and the church's role in reshaping it. Augustine was simply trying to reappropriate what he had learned from the Biblical prophets and early church fathers and other philosophical resources, in the context of this new cultural crisis. He capably showed his contemporaries that the church was not merely tied to a deteriorating political structure but that it had a role to play in the creation of a new human environment.

The intentional cadres of the emerging monastic movement played a key role in the mutation of Christianity from the Greco Roman to the medieval world. In one of the most creative moments of church history, monasticism expressed the determined, disciplined intent of the church to encounter the cultural challenge of northern Europe and try to tame this immense, vigorous revolutionary force. Missionaries were soon infiltrating the entire subcontinent of northern Europe to see if the church could relate itself creatively to the Teutonic world. As we look back on it now from a safe vantage point, some of us might regret some of the methods used to tame the Teutonic libido, but without these strong initiatives the Christian contribution to history might have been trapped in a rotting Roman box.

The third mutation we will mention, although there

were many intervening ones, had its setting in the sixteenth century. With its stress on the priesthood of all believers, justification by faith alone, and ecclesial experimentation, the Reformation embodied a new Christian style of life. It was not just a single mutation, but one that spawned many other mutations. It would be much too complicated to delve into the history of those subsequent mutations, either in Protestant or in Catholic ecclesiology, but suffice it to say that the last five centuries have been ones of accelerating mutation, and we are now standing at the peak of that acceleration process.

Shaped by its memory of God's action toward the people of Israel, the church is being freed in any new circumstance to reflect upon that circumstance in the light of God's previous action. Constantly we are experiencing the structures upon which we have relied being taken away from us. We meet the God of Israel as slayer of our obsolete social structures.

Biblical Patterns

Fittingly we conclude this discussion of existence as revolution by setting it within the framework of Biblical theology. For this historical pattern is not foreign to the Biblical witness. Rather it is in fact embedded in the entire Biblical saga and has most of its origins there. We will distill our discussion into four key examples of mutating religious structures in the Old Testament. Many other examples could be found both in the Old and New Testaments, but these four will suffice to illustrate the pattern: (1) Exodus, (2) Canaan, (3) Captivity, and (4) Hellenization.

1. The crisis of the exodus. The Hebrews had become enmeshed over a long period of time in Egyptian culture as a depressed minority, a slave people. In the transition into the wilderness, they had to decide what kind

of people they were to become. An entire cultural orientation was dying. They were in process of becoming "a people." But in the transition a crisis arose: many wanted to return to Egypt. After all, they knew what to expect there. They did not know what the wilderness would hold. It was threatening beyond imagination. It took all the resources of the best leadership of the Hebrews to negotiate that transition and to respond to that which they would understand as the call of Yahweh into exodus.

2. The next crisis was equally decisive. It involved the transition from being a mobile, bedouin, pastoral culture into a sedentary, less mobile, agricultural, and urban culture. The Hebrews stormed into Palestinian lands. Essentially a depressed minority, they now confronted a highly advanced society in Palestine: the Canaanites, who had grown out of the remarkable Phoenician culture. Canaan was a well-developed, literary, artistic society in comparison with the underdeveloped, nonliterary, bedouin tribesmen who were invading.

The question for Israel centered upon how they could live in Canaan and assimilate certain aspects of Canaanite technology and culture, without being seduced by what seemed to them a pagan, idolatrous understanding of religion. The prophetic tradition warned against amalgamation. Much interaction nonetheless ensued. The Canaanites taught the Hebrews much about becoming a civilized people. It was an immense cultural crisis. There were no simple answers. They had to decide contextually what was best. It required a mutation in religious and cultural consciousness.

3. Finally Israel established a monarchy. They developed a relatively stable system of government, administration of law, and priestly institution. But soon, after only a few generations of existing as a nation, their very national life was threatened. They now had territory. They had something to defend. They had a king. They

had a bureaucracy. The crisis came in the form of Assyrians and Babylonians—superior military powers, who sent them into bondage, a cultural crisis of incredible proportions. Their national identity and continuity was at stake. For generations they had to learn to live in Babylon. They tried to remember their former tradition but it was difficult. Their question was: If you cannot be in Jerusalem, how can you really remember and celebrate the deeds of Yahweh? The story of the sixth- and seventh-century B.C. Hebrew prophets is essentially the story of negotiating this cultural and religious mutation.

4. Soon after their return to Jerusalem from captivity, and the reinstatement of some semblance of stability and continuity in the Judaic tradition, came the challenge of Hellenization. The Jews were confronted not only with a foreign military power but much more subtly with a pervasive cultural challenge. Hellenization was to the Judaic world what secularization is today to the Christian world. It required essential modifications in the thought structures of Jewish faith.

These four moments of historical crisis and mutation, however briefly described, nonetheless serve to illustrate the fact that the religious tradition to which we are accountable and of which we are heirs has negotiated many profound crises and challenges, each of which demanded basic mutations, and each of which produced significant new insights into the faith of Israel.

That these are revolutionary times cannot be denied. Yet God is in the midst of the revolution. That reality to which the Judeo-Christian tradition has pointed with the term "God" is an active participant in the revolutionary process.

Most revolutionaries say: We must make revolutionary responses to these revolutionary times. The peculiar slant of our thesis is: The most appropriate response to revolutionary times is the recovery of a revolutionary tradition.

CHAPTER 9

Dying Forms of a Living Tradition

We exist today in the context of a living tradition which now is experiencing the senility and death of certain structures and viewpoints which once were at the center of that tradition. If the Christian tradition can be compared to a living organism which grows new cells and sheds old dysfunctional cells, we may say that its present condition is the conflict-filled stage of having to slough off once-living cells which are now dead weight on the living organism.

The cells being sloughed off are historically designated: pietism, denominationalism, and pragmatic activism. A certain sense of crisis and suspense now impinges on many local congregations and national bodies as these dysfunctional cells are being torn off the living organism, and one wonders how the continuing organism will function without them.

Since we are so poorly grounded in a historic awareness of past crises of the church, it is difficult to gain a larger perspective on our predicament or to perceive the vitality remaining within the total organism. It is much easier to see the painful process of senility and death of the old cells. Both our predicament and possibility may be captured in a single phrase: dying forms of a living tradition.

What are the essential features of the old self-understanding now being sloughed off?

1. The old image has been trapped in an obsolete compulsion to perpetuate *denominational* loyalties. The credibility of that image is increasingly doubtful. The emerging generation couldn't care less about denominational identifications.

2. Another dying cell is *pietism,* i.e., withdrawing into the safety and isolation of the good community that boasts of its moral and religious superiority over the surrounding world. Even in its liberalized forms, these pietistic elements have remained strong. The church often looks like an exodus from the world to which it is called in mission.[1] But this exodus is becoming harder to achieve and is increasingly being viewed as unfaithful to the church's essential nature and task.

3. Much of our immediate past has been dominated by a pragmatic understanding of the reality of the church. Under this image, the church was essentially an *activistic* community of doing, and its problems were all viewed fundamentally as organizational problems. It conceived of its task as the conversion of the world, by which it meant the ingesting of the digestible parts of the world into the denominational institutional structure. It too easily measured its vitality in numerical terms. It tried to get great numbers of people to ecclesial pep rallies with a great play of enthusiasm, friendliness, verve, and muscular Christianity. Whatever worked to attract people away from the world and into the church seemed good enough for pragmatic activism, however inadequately it might have measured up to the historic Christian tradition. With this pragmatic theology (no less theological for its unreflective character) it judged the adequacy of its behavior solely in terms of how successfully it was functioning toward enhancing organizational goals.[2]

Applying nothing but these old, increasingly senile images to assess the adequacy of the present-day church, it certainly seems to be faltering, failing to fulfill *these* particular goals. Many churchmen look with despair upon the scene today inasmuch as they understandably bring to it only these assumed standards of judgment. But under other images, such as an ecumenical, sacramental, or missional image of the nature of the church, the present plight of the church might not seem so hopeless, but rather very promising indeed.

Such is the old image, dominated by denominational defensiveness, pietistic withdrawal, and pragmatic activism. It is now clear that this old image, except for the formalities of a funeral, is dead. Put differently, God is already judging those institutional structures which our fathers have bequeathed us. The living Lord of history is saying No to our schismatic, pietistic activism. But where is the divine Yes being spoken?

It is understandable for us to become frustrated with these dying structures which have been shaped under a questionable image of the church. But it is now time for the renewing church to grasp more deeply than it has before that these are dying forms of a *living* tradition. If we had a keener historical consciousness, we would simultaneously be *more* capable of self-criticism and *less* vulnerable to despair over the present inadequacies of the church.

The viable alternatives may be boiled down to three basic options. It is as though the institutional church were now standing at a historic crossroads confronting three options: archaism, worldliness, and tradition. Those familiar with the inner conflicts within the church's leadership will readily recognize these options as embodied in various forms of leadership and ideology.

1. The first alternative is a wistful *archaism* whose only plea is for more activistic dedication to familiar

strategies. Many there are, especially among the settled leadership of the church, who can see in the other two alternatives only the collapse of the institutional structures to which they have been so faithfully devoted. The proponents of this alternative are keenly aware of the potential irrelevance of traditionalism or the threats to institutional stability in the alternative of worldliness. Besides, many older churchmen see nothing fundamentally wrong or inadequate about the old pietistic, introverted, activistic image of the passing period. Their answers to all the frustrations of the present are just what you would expect of those who know how to judge the church only by a quantitative, organizational, pragmatic standard. To them the answer is simply to organize better, recruit more loyal young leadership which is committed to the older image of the church, or at least unaware of the radical vulnerability of that image, and to build up a well-functioning organization using the methods of pragmatic activism which we all know so well. Many sincere church board members, churchly bureaucratic executives, and, above all, residential pastors are in this camp, to say nothing of vast numbers of regular every-Sunday laymen who are basically satisfied with the older image of the church and find no reason seriously to quarrel with it.

We are calling the first alternative "archaism," since its principal strategy in the face of the perplexing new mood of our time is simply to cling to old patterns, erstwhile reliable procedures, and familiar ideas. It is archaic because it is not really in touch with the newness of the present situation, and the questions it frames basically emerge out of an orientation once relevant but now obsolete. Although some proponents of this alternative are vocal, articulate, and determined, for the most part the strength of archaism is unconscious, sentimental, and below the level of awareness.

2. A second alternative, which might be called a holy *worldliness,* is based on a theology of secularization. Advocates of this alternative, whose voices are increasingly heard in national leadership, insist that the life of the church is in the midst of the secular structures instead of withdrawing into a religious womb. If the contemporary world is the scene of God's concrete self-disclosure, the church is called to awaken to this speech of God amid the secular realities of the world.[3] The clues for Christian self-understanding are to be taken from involvement, immersion in the life of the world, from contemporary art and politics, and the events of our time in which God's presence is incognito, instead of trying to perpetuate some clannish circle of piety.

This second alternative has much to commend it, and there is every reason to believe that this option is in the ascendancy in both Protestant and Catholic leadership today. But the laity as a whole stand before this option with considerable bewilderment. It seems more like dying than living.

3. The third option confronting the church is in one sense the most radical, but only because it is in a more profound sense the most conservative. For it points to the hope of the church as rerootage in the deeper *tradition* of the church's historic self-identity as the wellspring of relevant engagement in the world. This option differs radically from archaism in that it finds the larger ecumenical tradition in tension with the more recent nineteenth-century pragmatic, activistic, pietistic denominational traditions that archaism would seek to keep alive. Although it has much more in common theologically with what we are calling worldliness than it does with archaism, it differs from worldliness essentially at one crucial point: It celebrates God's self-disclosure as once for all made known in a history of salvation of which Jesus Christ is the center, and only then, and in the light of

that self-disclosure, is God's presence in the contemporary world knowable. This alternative would seek to allow the historic ecumenical tradition (Irenaeus, Augustine, Anselm, Aquinas, the Reformers, etc.) to stand in judgment both of our passing structures of piety and our contemporary forms of political, social, and philosophical understanding. It perceives the distortions of the church of pietistic liberalism more sympathetically in the context of its participation and continuity with the larger apostolic tradition.

If compelled to choose only one alternative, we would have to go with the third option, on the grounds that the historic tradition, when properly understood, will lead us precisely toward witness and service in the midst of the world, whereas worldliness per se will not necessarily lead us to the Christ event which enables us to understand the inner reality of the world. But fortunately our choice need not necessarily be one alternative to the exclusion of the others. Any one of the three options, if taken exclusively, rejecting the others, will lead to shortsightedness, if not disaster. The three options, and especially the last two, need the valid aspects of each other for their completion and correction. For worldliness or archaism without tradition would be centerless. Tradition or archaism without worldliness would be irrelevant. And there is a real sense in which neither tradition nor worldliness will be institutionally effective without maintaining some continuity with the pragmatic, institutional structures that archaism seeks to preserve. Let us spell this out further, by criticizing any exclusive strategy based solely on any one of the three alternatives.

1. Astute observers know that attempts to turn back the clock and resurrect a gung ho activism are almost certainly doomed to frustration in the light of the present mood of the emerging generation. Even in conservative parish situations, it is increasingly hard to achieve this

spirit of activism, and next to impossible in more urban, secularized settings. Although lip service may be given to the activistic ideals, it is like pulling eyeteeth to drum up the kind of program enthusiasm that would allow the vitality of unreflective activism to come alive.

2. The Achilles' heel of the worldly alternative is its temptation toward institutional and historical rootlessness. In its thrust toward experimentation, relevance, and presence in the world, it is tempted to have a premature amnesia toward the Judeo-Christian memory. As significant and exciting as the alternative of worldliness appears, it often lacks a sense of history and ecclesial self-identity in its headstrong plunge toward the world. One wonders whether the church is really prepared to live in that sense "in the world," inasmuch as it has not yet discovered who it is, either with respect to a firm churchly self-identity, or deep rootage in historic Christianity. All our missioning and engaging in dialogue with the world is centerless and pointless if we fail to discover who we are as a historic community in dialogue with the world. There is some validity to the suspicion that the Americanized version of Bonhoeffer's call to worldliness and religionless Christianity is merely another bourgeoisie version of culture-Protestantism, simply absorbing available cultural values into identification with the church's message, in full continuity with the accommodationist temptations of nineteenth-century Protestant liberalism.

3. Likewise an exclusive, overriding concern for tradition can lead to irrelevance and innocuousness, if not reappropriated in meaningful contemporary language and coupled with the call for radical experimentation. A tradition-oriented stance, however urgently needed today, stands in constant danger of a kind of fixation on the past which is not in the deeper sense faithful to the core of the historic Christian tradition itself.

If it should be the case, however, that the God who

makes himself known once for all in Jesus Christ, as mediated through the historic tradition, is the same God who speaks in the present moment through contemporary history and culture, and is knowable in the light of his self-disclosure in Christ, then the hiatus between tradition and worldliness would be overcome. This is precisely how we propose to bring together the seemingly opposite viewpoints of a now-oriented worldliness and a past-oriented tradition—theologically, by affirming that the speech of God in the now is fully understandable only from the vantage point of his speech in the history of the people of Israel and in Jesus Christ.

CHAPTER 10

Radical Theology
and the Institutional Church

We have seen how the tension between the church's internal reality and its visibility has plagued Christian theology from its beginning and even today remains a dilemma on our hands. We have explored the question of how institutional embodiment is a legitimate aspect of the church's destiny, and how institutional continuity might be sought amid a revolutionary historical context. One task remains untouched—the climate of contemporary theology. Where does theology stand today? What is its specific role amid the current crisis of institutional continuity?

We will focus on the notion of a "radical theology," which seems to gather under one umbrella many of the theological themes to which the underground church appeals. Many subterraneans view the current phase of theology as a radical one. It is just that assumption which we intend seriously to challenge, with the counterargument that theology today is not in a radical phase but rather in one of its more benign phases, partly because of its lack of attention to the very themes we have been discussing up to this point. It is benign because it has been willing to skirt the hard questions of concretizing Christian community historically and sociologically. It has tended toward innocuousness because it has given up

on the really demanding question of relating secularization and apostolicity. It is benign because it has bar-
gained with an esoteric spiritualizing ecclesiology that
fails to take seriously the grass-roots historical reality of
the church.

Radical theology, of course, is not a new term, and has
been utilized for many years with an entirely different
constellation of meanings.[1] Our purpose is to sharpen
up a more tough-minded definition of radical theology
so as to cut away its dull and unscandalous aspects. The
thesis is quite simple: that the one thing most conspicuously absent from much so-called "radical theology" is
genuine radicality.

The principal recent epiphany of genuine radical theology has been Bonhoeffer. None of the post-Bonhoefferian
developments have matched the intensity and depth of
his particular brand of radicalization of theology. What
made Bonhoeffer's theology radical? Merely his biography
and life commitment? Much more so it was his theology
that made his biography radical.

Bonhoeffer intensified the Barthian-Bultmannian radicalization by focusing directly at the most unexpected
point: *the worldliness of the Word of God.* If Barth was
concerned with the revelation of the Word, Bultmann
with the communication of the Word, Bonhoeffer was
essentially grasped by the worldliness of the Word of
God. On the basis of his high Christology and Barthian
dogmatic substructure, the most unexpected dimension
now emerged as the focus of radical theology: the secularizing world, the humanizing process as the arena of
Christ's Lordship, the maturing world as the new locus
where the Word of God is knowable, the celebration of
man's coming of age.[2]

Against two monstrous distortions Bonhoeffer struggled: on the one hand, pietistic withdrawal from the
world in introverted religiosity, and on the other hand,

an introverted secularism, a phony superficial humanism that exists in ignorance of its standing under the claim and judgment and grace of God in Jesus Christ. To know the world properly is to know it in Jesus Christ, and to know Christ is to know his involvement in the world.[3]

The deepest dimensions of Barth's radicalization of revelation and Bultmann's radicalization of kerygmatic preaching were internalized, assimilated, and reappropriated in Bonhoeffer's thought on the matured world. He lingers in our memory as the most dramatic prototype of radical theology because his radical life gave credence to his radical thought. Those who have castrated his theology by picking and choosing one or two sentences out of his prison letters which do not correspond with the total balance and range of his earlier thought have only temporarily succeeded in deradicalizing his worldliness—reducing it from a Christological worldliness to the cheap inverted worldliness against which he clearly protested in his posthumous writings. They have taken the secular less serious than God himself takes it in Jesus Christ.

In contrast, the pseudo radicalism of much recent self-conscious "revolutionary" theology reminds us of the pseudo-revolutionary style of the Daughters of the American Revolution and their un-Boston tea parties. We refer specifically to their elitist, pretentious, introverted character, and their comically exaggerated sense of *now* being a part of a revolution that has already happened over a century ago. This sort of alleged radicalism is little more than another verse of the repetitious chorus of culture-Protestantism, the uncritical absorption of prevailing cultural motifs into the Christian ethos, baptizing whatever one imagines to be happening in history as Christian.[4]

God's own worldly engagement is the subject of genuine

radical theology. When that tension is reduced, theology is deradicalized.

However innocuous and nonrevolutionary the "death of God" or "death of the church" movements might look in relation to a genuinely radical theology, today we are being required to ask, where do we go from here? Whatever ambiguities may characterize the new theological mood, we must now ask the more substantive question: What is the special opportunity being offered contemporary theology in the ensuing decade, in the aftermath of the "death of God" and "death of the church" episodes?[5]

Theology in just this context is being given a new opportunity to speak in a more penetrating way than it had been able to speak in the previous decade. Although many of us might have preferred to have gone blandly along in the paths of the theological currents of the decade prior to the "Christian atheists" and guerrilla churchmen, we must now confess that we are being called by their initiatives to a tougher task of deeper reflection and clearer communication. We can rejoice that we have been stung and shocked out of our drowsiness and complacency. Theology has taken a sharp, unexpected, yet hopeful turn.

In our new situation, we are now being forced into much more primal theological territory. We are being confronted with the much more profound question of the *reality* of God and the *reality* of the *ecclesia*. How are we to speak the name "God" in our time and respond to the reality of God in community? This is the nub of the question that faced the people of Israel at one primitive point in their history: Who is the One who meets us concretely in history? We dare not give him a name. Perhaps we must only use some sort of cryptic symbol in our time, as the Hebrews resorted to the verbal sign YHWH. The point is, we are being forced to that primitive level of theological accountability. What does it mean to say "God" or YHWH? This is not merely the question of our attempt to speak in ways that communicate with modern man—these are wholly secondary issues to the primordial question of the reality of God himself.[6] This is what we are learning in this new era of theological history. The new situation is forcing us back into that embryonic, fundamental level of theology itself.

To affirm the positive potentialities of our new situation, however, is not to ignore the limitations that have fallen upon us. In some ways the "death of God" and "death of the church" movements have made our task much more difficult. To many, theology has always meant at worst a dangerous threat to the truth of the faith or at best an ivory-tower irrelevance. Both pietists and accommodationists have every reason to seize upon any available opportunity to dismiss theology as such, and especially a genuinely missional theology that has long challenged both pietism and accommodation.

Many of us have been struggling in the context of grass-roots pietistic liberalism for a good while now, and at last we had begun in the last two decades to get beyond the limited stance of having continually to defend theology as a legitimate servant of the church. In fact we were beginning to move into a decisively offensive thrust in which theology was beginning to be taken seriously by a renewing laity. We were beginning to see all around us small disciplined groups emerging which were committed to lucid study of the Biblical witness and the historic tradition, relevant dialogue with the world, the renewal of the liturgy, and the development of ordered communities of mission in the world. This was happening both within and without the ordinary residential parish structures, and it was happening under the aegis of what you might call a latent theological consensus.[7]

During that period of rather inconspicuous academic theology in America, we witnessed the beginning of a profound theological renewal within the laity, and an intensive search for missionary structures for the congregation.[8]

It was into just this promising context that the "death of God" and "death of the church" movements entered as a disturbing, provocative intrusion, an upsetting of that consensus. Unquestionably the real powder keg was set off by the "death of God" and "death of the church" initiatives, which sent that consensus splintering off into a million parts, and now, to put it mildly, contemporary theology is up for grabs. Nobody knows where it is going. There are no solidified schools. There are only loose ends lying around. We feel as though we have been bombed.

It is precisely within this context that we wish to propose a redefined understanding of authentic *radical* theology. Let us claim that term and press it to its depth, hoping to reengage theology in the kind of radical human questioning under which genuine theology has always understood itself to be placed, centering in our attempt to grasp our human condition as having been grasped by God himself. There are some in our generation who are capable, determined, and willing to reassert and renew that tradition of genuine radical theology in which the radical element unapologetically is the tension between the revelation of God and the secularizing world.

The promising thing about contemporary theology is that the "Christian atheists" have boldly uncorked the most exciting new possibility of dealing directly with the genuinely radical questions of theology—the questions of the reality of God, the self-disclosure of God, the worldliness of God, and the embodiment of the people of God in living communities of reconciliation. We have Bill

Hamilton and Stephen Rose and many others to thank for helping us to make that clear. But they have not given us a radical theology, only the possibility for it.

The most promising task at the moment is just the one that may seem least obvious to us: to move toward a consistent solidification of the best themes of twentieth-century theology in its profoundest radicalism and to test its charisma to see whether it can be given institutional embodiment. Radical theology is moving into its severest testing phase. It is being required by history to try to embody itself in living communities of faith and witness and service, so as to make some continuing contribution to history. This calls us to the innovative task of new institution-building, which will require organizational acumen, patience, and above all, hope.

In a deeper sense, however, we are not merely proposing a task ahead for the future, but reporting on what is already happening in many experimental centers for church renewal and live parishes currently involved in relevant mission. While it cannot be our purpose now to review these experiments, we can at least point the reader to several recent discussions that clarify the directions now being taken. Among the best are William Holmes's *The Cosmopolitan Community,* David Schuller's *Emerging Shapes of the Church,* and the literature of Chicago's Ecumenical Institute.

In many such communities the renewing church is already being intentionally embodied in new sociological structures for mission. Radical theology today is being called to exist as a servant to the *de facto* renewal of the church, and not merely its promised, potential renewal.

To work toward better institutionalization in mission is not to seek a dampening of charisma, but a means of manifesting it. This is the hard question before a genuinely radical theology—Can it be embodied?

Chapter 11

The Social Welfare State: A Changing Context for a Changing Mission

The new sociopolitical context of the welfare state surprisingly outmodes the individualistic conception of witness and service that has been prevalent in much recent social activist literature.[1] Much of the *avant-garde* strategy that has enamored the social action establishment during the last twenty years is being rapidly outmoded by political events. Our thesis: The renewing church should accept not merely the idea but the reality of the welfare state, and not try to perform a host of governmental functions which it has been trying to do rather ineffectively through private charity. The mutating church is being freed to give its attention to its central vocation in history of witnessing to the gospel of God's saving action in Jesus Christ. Although this witness must be validated by service, the church's activism is cheap and phony without clear and meaningful witness.

The social gospel movement recognized the wretched indebtedness of pietism to a capitalistic structure with its great immoral concentrations of wealth.[2] It viewed the whole strategy of philanthropy not only as a totally inadequate solution, but also as an immoral apology for deteriorating capitalism. The social gospel movement advanced the awareness of the church's social mission a great deal by awakening the church to the injustices in which it participated. It pointed to social problems that did not admit of solutions through mere private philanthropy, e.g., war and peace, racial injustice, social security, etc. In the social gospel movement we see an increasing involvement of the Christian community in the political decision-making process, attempting to influence governmental structures to improve social environments.

History has moved at a rapid pace since the 1930's, when this country began to move decisively toward the welfare state. Many churchmen have resisted the socializing process, associating political responsibility with individual freedom, and an absence of governmental interference.

The central fact that we want to assert as a *de facto* reality today is: *We live in a welfare state.* Whether one likes that or not is beside the point. Whether one might have applauded or opposed the welfare state, one cannot deny that we now live in it and will continue to. There is no way to turn the clock back to private charity and individualistic philanthropy. The state has already assumed many of the responsibilities that the social gospel wanted the church to be doing. The government has become broadly concerned with social security, hospitalization for the aged, and welfare programs for the poor. It takes care of the widow and the fatherless, gives child dependency aid, etc.

Curiously enough the social gospel tradition has been much more successful than it usually gives itself credit for in the building of the welfare state. It is not implausible to regard the welfare state as, in a large measure, the indirect achievement of a liberal Christian tradition that was at first seeking private solutions to social problems. It is as if having pounded on the door of the conscience of democratic society for many decades to awaken it to the human needs of the poor, that society finally has at long last come to care, to some extent, about whether people are hungry, have jobs, decent living conditions, and equal justice under the law.

If so, what is our problem now? In its commitment to social change and its polemic against individualistic pietism, the church of the social gospel tended to neglect its crucial task of credible *witness* to Jesus Christ and to the saving action of God in history. Ironically, it became fixated upon a social activism that did not differ all that much from the pietistic activism of the generation against which it was rebelling.

The pathos of the social gospel movement as it exists today in a welfare state is simply this: As governmental social welfare increases, it leaves the social gospel churchman with increasingly less to do which can be clearly distinguished as Christian action. What happens when everybody has adequate housing, medical care, pensions, plenty of leisure time, etc.? To illustrate: For decades the social gospel movement has worked hard with the labor movement in trying to help workers to develop bargaining skills. What happens after they organize and become fat members of the establishment with plenty of social security and the backbone of an introverted, selfish affluent society? This is the malaise of the heirs of the social gospel movement. This condition has bred a peculiar strain of social activists who sometimes entangle themselves in curious subcultural alliances because it seems that that is the only way to keep the church alive, according to a social action definition.

Since we already live in the era of the welfare state in which the government is increasingly taking over charitable and social welfare functions, the lucid church can merely acknowledge that as a fact and not struggle against it. Instead it is now free to call the government to its responsibilities in social care, and to become itself a model of genuine human community.

Now we come to another heuristic thesis: The church is being freed by the success of the welfare state to focus anew upon its more crucial, more indispensable vocation of witness to Jesus Christ. Our caveat is: Quit trying to make the church do what the government does better. One example: As an expression of social concern, the church has become involved in spending large quantities of money in building homes for the aged. These are excellent homes, and in fact many are so luxurious that often only wealthy people can live in them—an appalling moral embarrassment to the churches. We have built church-related "charities" that poor people really cannot afford, a curious exercise in so-called philanthropy. Yet, ironically while the church was building affluent elderly citizens' homes, the government was also very much involved in it and on a much broader scale, and did a much more equitable job of it. The message the church is getting from history at this point is: Get out of the private welfare business. Call the government to its social welfare vocation to care for society. Churchmen must continue to be involved politically to encourage appropriate political action. But we must now recognize that the very success of the welfare state is liberating, since the church is now free from many of these absorbing and time-consuming tasks of social welfare administration. It is now free to work harder to build innovative models of authentic community, and to articulate its witness to God's saving action in history in the language of our day.

Finally a dissenting opinion on the relation of witness and service.[3] Individualistic pietism stressed witness. The social gospel has emphasized service. The missional church today needs to focus not exclusively on service but on a serious, new, profound, determined engagement with the issues of straightforward Christian *witness.* We are not proposing this from the viewpoint of individualistic pietism, but rather from a full and joyous affirmation of the welfare state. To say that the greater need of our time is witness does not mean to ignore the urgent need for service. People remain hungry and dehumanized. The church must continue to work for the poor, and claim the consciences of those who are responsible for caring politically and economically for the dispossessed. But we face constantly a choice of priorities.

The state cannot make the church's witness, but it can do its service. Only the church can make its witness. That is why the priority in our time can and should shift to witness. A priority does not mean an exclusive emphasis, neglecting the works of love. One's witness is phony unless that witness is embodied in serving deeds.

"Giving a cup of cold water in the name of Christ" is an appropriate image of the interrelation of witness and service. Individualistic pietism tended insensitively to witness to Christ without the cup of cold water. Some recent activism has tended unreflectively to give the cup of cold water, but without knowing how to articulate the motivating basis of its service.

The witnesssing and serving church in the midst of the welfare state must learn to give the cup of cold water in a new form: through the social welfare establishment. That is how we now must in large part render our tithe of service to man, as over against individualistic philanthropy. But in a deeper sense we must learn how to witness if we are really to serve the modern world.

Many young clergymen despair over the church because it does not now seem to have any significant piece of the action in the welfare establishment. So we find the curious anomaly of pastors who have committed themselves essentially to a serving ministry informed by a social gospel theology, who, after having preached a few years, decide to join the fight against poverty or to get into community organization or join the Peace Corps or begin a teaching ministry. Much of this despair over the church is due to a theological failure to redefine Christian mission in the social welfare state. Obviously the church is not doing as spectacularly as governmental programs are in social service because we are living in the welfare state in which the government quite properly, and often under the guidance of Judeo-Christian conscience, has undertaken its duties of concern for the poor, the unemployed, the needy, etc. But it is a tragedy that we have not yet developed a conception of the witnessing ministry that would legitimize the task of the proclaiming church in and of itself without the social welfare crutch. For many, witness seems to be such a petty and secondary thing to be doing, when one could be doing service.

In the secularizing world, service is finally simpler and easier than witness. Usually it is stated the other way around, that anybody can talk about high ideals but it is much more difficult to go out and enact them in service. Today, however, it may be easier to give the cup of cold water than to give it in the name of Christ; easier to work on low-income housing than to explain why the action of God in history motivates one to serve the poor by working on low-income housing; easier to do things in service than to reflect on the motivation of one's doing.

To draw a dichotomy, as some do, between choosing the world *or* the church (or between a theology of the church *or* a secular theology) is an utterly unacceptable framing of the question. There can be no adequate theology of the church which does not grapple with the reality of the world to which it is called in service and witness. But equally, one can say there can be no adequate theology of the world without the church, which witnesses to the world of its own inner meaning, intention, and significance.

The way to love the world is not to emasculate the church, drive it out of the world, or separate it from the world. The best gift the church can proffer to the world is to be the church, to fulfill its mission of love, hope, and reconciliation.

The most serious way to affirm the world is to affirm it as having itself been affirmed by God. This is precisely the function of the church. The church (when it is being itself) is that community which holds before the *saeculum* its own authentic being and honors the world in its deepest sense as itself having been honored by God in its creation and redemption.

There are some who suggest that the church simply cannot survive as a continuing institution in the emerging world. Much talk of "religionless Christianity" and "churchless Protestantism" may be whistling in the dark, attempting honorifically to reassure the church that even though it will not have institutional form, it will nevertheless have some sort of vague meaning as a disembodied reality. It is against just that spirit, however well intentioned, that we are now struggling. Without palpable embodiment, the church is merely an idea in our heads.

Some expect the church to fold, others are convinced that it has already folded. We are convinced that the church will live in the modern world so long as God intends to declare himself to the world and make his love known. But the self-disclosure of the living God in history is always surprising to our duller, less radical expectations of religion and cultus. Just such a painful correction of our expectations is taking place in this generation.

Since God does will to make himself known, the church will exist. Wherever it exists, it will continue to be embodied, visibly structured in some way, either archaically or relevantly in the emerging world. The question for us is not whether, but how the church will be embodied— whether in quaint vestigial anachronisms or as a community of celebration of the love of God and man.

Institutional Reform in the 1970's

Although it has not been our primary purpose to announce programmatic proposals for reform, this discussion seems incomplete without some attempt to clarify where we go from here in institutional reconstruction. While we do not intend to give sustained attention to detailed proposals, we do think it is only fair to the reader to give him at least some hint of the direction of the reforms that will be demanded in this decade.

Clearly the only hope for institutional continuity lies in institutional change. We are not speaking of a static, but a mobile, continuity. If the institutional church is to be something more than sheer vestigial archaism, then it must be reshaped.

We will mention only seven specific goals for institutional change in the 1970's, aware that many others could be articulated with equal persuasiveness. Even these seven we will not spell out in detail, but merely list them as urgent objectives, admitting that the strategies for achieving these goals will remain highly debatable.

1. The church must grow out of its outdated indebtedness to a slave image of *woman*. The role of women in the church must change from the feminine religious mystique to that of full participation in adult decision-making. The church must share in the new generation's

hope for a humanization of woman. This must be done not only by encouraging women to take leadership roles in policy making, but more so by striving to embody model forms of human community in which woman is seen not as a sexual being alone but as a human being.

2. We are being called into a difficult period of *the ecumenizing of our ecclesial institutions.* This will doubtless be a painfully difficult task, exacerbated in part by the fact that many people are no longer interested in it. Too many otherwise responsible renewalists have already given up on actually building ecumenical institutions. If the body of Christ is one, however, we are called to seek persistently for an institutional embodiment of that oneness, despite the frustrating obstacles of vested interests, sentiment, and ideological rigidity.

To be effective, the ecumenizing process must take grass-roots institutional shape. We are past the point of thinking of ecumenicity merely as a formal negotiation of ecclesiastical big shots in a distant city. This decade will be a time of reconceiving each motive, each alternative, and each action of the local church in an ecumenical framework. This does not imply that the current denominational structures are completely dysfunctional. In fact, a major task of ecumenizing will be to discover how the best aspects of the varying traditions can be brought constructively into the ecumenical whole.

3. Representative bodies must become more fairly representative. One reason for the development of the public demonstration and protest style of encounter politics is that the establishment has not taken sufficient initiative within itself to *reform its own representational systems,* so as to make itself more inclusive and fair to those left out.

In hoping for a better form of representative democracy, we trust that these more fairly based representative bodies would then act courageously so as not to be easily intimidated by vocal minorities who claim specific charisma and press unnegotiable demands. This decade will see increasing challenges from the radical confrontationists who will quickly presume to speak for the "true" church even though no one elected them to do so. The deliberative bodies are being forced to learn better to distinguish between true and false prophets. The best defense against irresponsible, anarchic pyrotechnics, however, is a truly representative process in which opportunity for dissent will itself be structured into the established procedures.

4. This decade demands an urgent *mission to youth culture,* a specific and intentional address of the Christian tradition to the emerging generation, of the same scope and style as the intensive missional effort of the nineteenth century to the underdeveloped, colonial peoples. The analogy could be drawn between:

Era:	late 19th century	late 20th century
Theology:	liberalizing pietism	secularizing theology
Agents:	foreign missionaries	new apostles to youth
Scope:	the non-Christian world	newly emerging world
Intent:	conversion	witness and service

If a serious mission to youth culture is attempted, it has many implications for institutional change in the church: the mission must be funded, the risk of dialogue must be taken, youth themselves must formulate the missional effort, the language and idiom of the new generation must be the means of communication, and most of this will have to happen outside of the walls of the present institution, since youth are already persuaded that the church belongs to a passing era.

The task is just as demanding today to speak to our own alienated youth culture, as it was previously to speak to alien non-Western cultures. The same quality of commitment and energy is demanded. The institutional church must shift its money and energies away from converting nonbelievers of other cultures to addressing the disenchanted sons of so-called Christian culture. If this can be meaningfully done in American society where technology and youth culture are far advanced, it could become a plausible pattern for other societies who will pass down the same road soon after we do.

5. The institutional church needs a communications revolution, or perhaps better said, it needs to share more deliberately in the communications revolution of our time. This is demanded on at least two crucial levels:

a. *Group processes.* Much has been discovered in sensitivity training, group therapy, and group dynamics about the nature of human communication, which needs better to be utilized in the reconstruction of the church. The basic encounter life-style is already recognizably akin to the pietistic tradition. Its strategy for human renewal is noticeably similar to the strategies of Protestant and Catholic pietism, with an emphasis upon open self-disclosure, self-examination, honest confession, conversion to a new life-style, awareness of others' feelings, the redemptive community, small-group experiencing of mutual pastoral care, etc. The analogy between T-groups and Wesleyan "bands" and other pietistic models is striking and suggestive. The latter-day inheritors of these pietistic traditions, however, have much to learn from the more adequate understanding of group processes only recently achieved by the behavioral sciences. Institutional reform should allow that knowledge to influence and reshape the very nature of our developing institutions. Accordingly, church reform should be a dialogical process, instead of an authoritarian plan through a chain of command.

b. Another aspect of the needed communications revolution is in the rediscovery of *worship* in credible contemporary images. The service of Christian worship deserves to become more of an actual happening—a total, visual, environmental, experiential happening, bringing various media of communication to bear upon the acts of confession, thanksgiving, and commitment. In an era in which minds shaped by electronic media have a very low tolerance for linear, didactic, propositional preaching or lecturing, the church's educational mission must learn to make use of the new technologies of communication in the service of Christian celebration.

6. The establishment must *spawn experimentation* at every level. Experimentation is not inimical to institutional continuity, but necessary for it. Those truly interested in institutional continuity will not be committed merely to maintaining institutions in their present form but to reshaping them so they can be transmitted to the next generation. This requires imaginative innovation in mission, education, social service, and leadership development. Institutionally this means that the church must be willing to fund experimentation, and the leadership must be willing to risk supporting forms of brainstorming that will challenge the very foundation on which it stands.

The other side is that the experimentation is called to stand in serious dialogue with the Christian tradition. If the experimentation does not take seriously the tradition and attempt to reappropriate it in some kind of meaningful categories, then it cannot expect to be funded by the institutional church—and should not—it should get its funds somewhere else. Ironically the most radical forms of experimentation today are those which dig deepest into the resources of the Western Christian tradition to enliven it for humanization of men today. Tradition and experimentation are far from antithetical.

The renewing church and the institutional church need each other in order to fulfill their mission. For how can the ordinary local parish continue authentically without some missional engagement and experimentation?

And how can the renewing, experimenting church maintain apostolic continuity and history identity without
some kind of dialogue with its immediate past and with
its larger ecumenical past? Each is unfulfilled without the
other.

7. A final need in institutional reform is to be aware
of *the limitations of institutional reform itself.* Merely
tinkering with the machinery is not going to solve the
deeper dilemmas of the Christian community in the
modern world. Stated more positively, the church is being called to a renewal of its inner life, to a reappropria-
tion of the best resources of the Christian tradition in
contemporary language, to a new spiritual depth that
will form the basis upon which we may be able to negotiate spiritually the suffering and cultural shock that we
will have to endure in this decade. Transition involves
suffering. Radical transition involves deep suffering of
the spirit, but also a possibility for extraordinary spiritual
growth.

Even at its best, the 1970's will be tough to negotiate
spiritually. Even if this decade is as smooth as could
possibly be envisioned—without war or a major political
catastrophe—the church will still undergo a profound
form of suffering which in Biblical terms would be called
a chastisement for idolatry. But if history is less kind to
us in the 1970's—if, for example, we have a major erup-
tion of violence, nuclear war, or chemical war, or deeper
forms of internal deterioration in our own society and in
ourselves, or if we should experience violent political
revolution that would literally tear the church away from
its dependence upon capitalistic society, then the church
would face the most profound form of cultural suffering.
In order to respond creatively to that suffering, it must be
in touch with the spiritual resources of the revolution-
izing Judeo-Christian tradition.

Perhaps it will require a profound experience of cultural loss, however, for us even to recognize these spiritual foundations, as it has so many times before in man's previous history. The deepest wellsprings of the Biblical faith may remain out of reach until we experience the painful probings of societal grief. So we are not speaking merely of the reshuffling of petty power in external institutional reform. More so we are looking forward to a fresh new human rediscovery of the love of God embodied in human community, and a risking trust in the final One who stands beyond the gods of Western society.

The church, like her Lord, has no place to lay her head in the world, because she does not belong *to* the world, although she certainly belongs *in* it. Her only authentic security is found in moving through the world, as it were in a pilgrim existence, trusting in the One who calls her both out of and into the world.

To speak of the hope of the church is to speak of our hope in the One who calls the church into being. Should our hope in this final reality turn out to be secure and well founded, then we could speak more assuredly about the hope we have for the church. Doubtless if our hope for the church in the modern world is based finally on our hope in human ingenuity in organization, or human courage in action, or human skill in communication, or the persistence of our sociological patterns, then surely our hope is in vain. But the authentic hope of the church consists strictly in the possibility and actuality of God's action in today's world and his will to raise the church up anew.

The church is only dead when the God who chooses to call it into being is dead. Since God lives there is hope for the church—perhaps not for the church in the particular forms we in the twentieth century have become accustomed narrowly to regard as "normal" for the life of the church. But for the church through which God chooses to continue his ministry to the world, there is no good reason for despair. Since the church exists as a response to the grace of God which is eternally revealed, the possibility of its renewal is never a closed case, any more than the crucifixion made Jesus of Nazareth a closed case.

Notes

PREFACE

1. Michael Novak, "The Revolution of 1976," *Commonweal,* Vol. LXXXVI, No. 16 (July 14, 1967), p. 441.

2. Charles Davis, *A Question of Conscience* (Harper & Row, Publishers, Inc., 1967); Stephen Rose (ed.), *Who's Killing the Church?* (Chicago City Missionary Society, 1966), pp. 8 ff.; James A. Pike, "Why I'm Leaving the Church," *Look,* April 29, 1969, pp. 54–58.

Chapter 1 ON ECCLESIAL PATRICIDE

1. For further discussion of a prognosis, see: Michael Novak, *A Time to Build* (The Macmillan Company, 1967), "Christianity: Renewed or Slowly Abandoned?" pp. 17 ff.; H. J. Blackham, *Religion in a Modern Society* (London: Constable & Co., Ltd., 1966), "The Present Status of Religion," pp. 104 ff.; Gerhard Szczesny, *The Future of Unbelief* (George Braziller, Inc., 1961), esp. "Christianity, An Early Theology Perpetuated," pp. 27 ff.; John Foster, *Requiem for a Parish* (The Newman Press, 1962); Gabriel Vahanian, *The Death of God: The Culture of Our Post-Christian Era* (George Braziller, Inc., 1961).

2. For a variety of discussions of these issues, see: Stephen Rose, *The Grass Roots Church* (Abingdon Press, 1966), pp. 121 ff.; Pierre Berton, *The Comfortable Pew* (J. B. Lippincott Company, 1965); David Poling, *The Last Years of the Church* (Doubleday & Company, Inc., 1969); Mary Jean Irion, *From*

the Ashes of Christianity: A Post-Christian View (J. B. Lippincott Company, 1968); Eberhard Stammler, *Churchless Protestantism* (The Westminster Press, 1964); Malcolm Boyd (ed.), *The Underground Church* (Sheed & Ward, Inc., 1968); Robert Adolfs, *The Grave of God* (Harper & Row, Publishers, Inc., 1966).

3. On the relation of bureaucratic power structures to the renewal of the church, see Gayraud S. Wilmore, *The Secular Relevance of the Church* (The Westminster Press, 1962), Ch. III, "The Faithful Use of Power"; Walter Muelder, "Power Structures, Ethical Concerns and the Church in the World," *Laity* 14 (Geneva: World Council of Churches), pp. 29–39; Report on *Institutionalism,* Montreal Faith and Order paper No. 37, pp. 1–29.

4. Emil Brunner, e.g., argues that "the body of Christ is a pure communion of persons entirely without institutional character" (*The Misunderstanding of the Church* [London: Lutterworth Press, 1952], pp. 10, 16–17, 74).

5. For a penetrating clarification of "The Two Aspects of the One Church," see Henri DeLubac, S.J., *The Splendour of the Church* (Sheed & Ward, Inc., 1956), pp. 55 ff.; also Hans Küng, *Truthfulness: The Future of the Church* (Sheed & Ward, Inc., 1968), pp. 32–42; for an excellent discussion of "The Christological Analogy," see Colin W. Williams, *The Church* (New Directions in Theology Today, Vol. IV) (The Westminster Press, 1968), pp. 71 ff.; Allan R. Brockway, *The Secular Saint* (Doubleday & Company, Inc., 1968), pp. 169 ff.

6. Perry London, *The Modes and Morals of Psychotherapy* (Holt, Rinehart and Winston, Inc., 1964); Hobart Mowrer, *The New Group Therapy* (D. Van Nostrand Company, Inc., 1965); William Glasser, *Reality Therapy* (Harper & Row, Publishers, Inc., 1965); E. Lakin Phillips and Daniel N. Wiener, *Short-Term Psychotherapy and Structured Behavior Change* (McGraw-Hill Book Company, Inc., 1966); Eric Berne, *Transactional Analysis in Psychotherapy* (Grove Press, Inc., 1961). Psychotherapy is undergoing an important revolution today, unrecognized by many who are not closely in touch with the field. Older therapies dominated by the Freudian tradition are being abandoned because of their inefficiency and mythological confusions. Behaviorists are pointing to the therapeutic possi-

bilities of social control. They are talking about commitment to community as the basis of health, and interpersonal integrity as the basis of therapeutic change. They speak of responsibility as the prototypical form of healthy human relationship. Eric Berne's theory of transactional analysis emphasizes our accountability to one another through our implicit "contracts." A growing group of "action therapists" are concerned not with achieving depth insights but with short-term behavioral changes that are geared into community structures and social controls (London, Phillips and Wiener).

7. Ernst Käsemann, *Essays on New Testament Themes* (London: SCM Press, Ltd., 1964), pp. 63–95.

8. Davis, *op. cit.*, p. 267. The notion of "creative disaffiliation" was introduced by Harvey Cox in *The Secular City* (The Macmillan Company, 1965), p. 230.

9. Davis, *op. cit.*, pp. 78 f.

Chapter 2 THE INSTITUTIONAL CHURCH AND REVOLUTIONARY CHANGE

1. Peter Berger's work is especially illuminating on this point. See *The Precarious Vision* (Doubleday & Company, Inc., 1961), Parts II and III, and *The Social Construction of Reality*, with Thomas Luckmann (Doubleday & Company, Inc., 1966), pp. 45 ff.

2. For a brilliant discussion of the issues of the church's unity and continuity "within a non-doctrinal framework," see James M. Gustafson, *Treasure in Earthen Vessels: The Church as a Human Community* (Harper & Brothers, 1961), p. ix, and *passim*. See also Küng, *op. cit.*, pp. 91 ff.

3. F. H. Allport, *Institutional Behavior* (The University of North Carolina Press, 1933); R. M. MacIver, *Society: A Textbook for Sociology* (Farrar & Rinehart, Inc., 1939); H. Gerth and C. W. Mills, *Character and Social Structure: The Psychology of Social Institutions* (Harcourt, Brace & Co., Inc., 1953); R. C. Angell, *The Integration of American Society: A Study of Groups and Institutions* (McGraw-Hill Book Company, Inc., 1941).

4. Joyce O. Hertzler, *American Social Institutions* (Allyn & Bacon, Inc., 1961), p. 84.

5. Talcott Parsons, *The Social System* (The Free Press of Glencoe, Inc., 1951); E. C. Hughes, "Institutions and the Community," in *Principles of Sociology*, ed. by A. M. Lee (Barnes & Noble, Inc., 1951), pp. 230 ff.; R. C. Angell, *Free Society and Moral Crisis* (University of Michigan Press, 1958), pp. 299 ff.

6. Hertzler, *op. cit.*, p. 85.

7. *Ibid.*, p. 91.

8. "Institution," *Oxford English Dictionary*, Vol. V, p. 354.

9. Leslie Paul, "The Church as an Institution—Necessities and Dangers," *Journal of Ecumenical Studies*, Vol. 4, No. 2 (Spring, 1967), p. 269.

10. Baron Friedrich von Hügel, *Essays and Addresses on the Philosophy of Religion* (E. P. Dutton & Company, Inc., 1926), "On the Place and Function, Within Religion, of the Body, of History, and of Institutions," pp. 57 ff.

Chapter 3 THE SEARCH FOR A NEW ESTABLISHMENT

1. The essay by Gustafson, *Treasure in Earthen Vessels*, comes closest to being a serious answer to that call, although it does not focus on a theology of the institutional church, but rather upon a nondoctrinal investigation of the human dimensions of the church.

2. David M. Paton (ed.), *The Old and the New in the Church* (London: SCM Press, Ltd., 1961), p. 79.

3. Cf. *Report: The United States Conference on Church and Society* (National Council of Churches, 1968), esp. pp. 16–20. This report is a compendium of strategies, long-range objectives, proximate objectives, targets, and tactics designated by participants in the Detroit Conference, October, 1967. Although it does not come to the issues of social strategy with a firm consensus on the nature of the church, it nevertheless is to be commended for its deliberate concern for strategy.

4. That this is not a new insight for recent thinking on church and society may be seen by examining some of the earlier treatments of this theme; cf. Shirley Jackson Case, *Christianity in a Changing World* (Harper & Brothers, 1941); Sherwood Eddy, *Revolutionary Christianity* (Willett, Clark & Company, 1939); Walter Rauschenbusch, *Christianity and the Social Crisis* (Association Press, 1912).

5. Cf. Jer., chs. 39; 50 to 52; The Lamentations of Jeremiah; Amos, chs. 1 to 3; The Book of Joel; Isa., chs. 10 to 25; Ps. 90.

6. Eric Hoffer, *The True Believer* (The New American Library, Inc., 1958), p. 20.

7. Jürgen Moltmann, *Theology of Hope* (Harper & Row, Publishers, Inc., 1967), Ch. 1.

8. Hoffer, *op. cit.*, pp. 25 ff.

9. Of course, for many the total rejection of the past is not an implication of the idea of revolution, but there are enough for whom such an implication does exist that we must not hold back our caveat against the abuse of a theology of revolution.

10. Paul, *loc. cit.*, pp. 276 f.

11. *The Port Huron Statement* (Students for a Democratic Society, 1964).

12. Martin E. Marty, *The Search for a Usable Future* (Harper & Row, Publishers, Inc., 1969), on "risk," pp. 141–146.

Chapter 4 ON QUITTING THE CHURCH

1. Davis, *op. cit.*; Stephen Rose (ed.), *Who's Killing the Church?*; Pike, *loc. cit.*

2. Much of our thinking on "plausibility" is indebted to Peter Berger's incisive analyses, esp. *The Sacred Canopy* (Doubleday & Company, Inc., 1967); cf. *The Precarious Vision*.

3. Eberhard Müller, *Die Welt ist anders geworden* (Hamburg: Furche Verlag, 1955).

4. Thomas Luckmann, *The Invisible Religion* (The Macmillan Company, 1967), pp. 28 ff.

5. John A. T. Robinson, *On Being the Church in the World* (The Westminster Press, 1960); Lesslie Newbigin, *The Household of God* (London: SCM Press, Ltd., 1957); J. R. Nelson, The Realm of Redemption (London: The Epworth Press, Publishers, 1951); George W. Webber, *God's Colony in Man's World* (Abingdon Press, 1960); Yves Congar, *Lay People in the Church* (The Newman Press, 1965).

6. For a survey of recent literature, see Thomas Oden, "Laity and Vocation: A Review Article," *Encounter,* Vol. 26 (Summer, 1965).

7. Herbert Marcuse, *Eros and Civilization* (Beacon Press, Inc., 1966).

8. Friedrich Gogarten, *Der Mensch zwischen Gott und Welt* (Friedrich Vorwork, 1956).

9. Denis de Rougemont, *The Christian Opportunity*, tr. by Donald Lehmkuhl (Holt, Rinehart and Winston, Inc., 1963), "The End of Pessimism," pp. 158 ff.

Chapter 5 QUESTIONS FOR SUBTERRANEANS

1. Davis, *op. cit.*, p. 42.

2. *Ibid.*, p. 40.

3. James Dittes, *The Church in the Way* (Charles Scribner's Sons, 1967); Gregory Baum, *The Credibility of the Church Today* (Herder & Herder, Inc., 1968).

4. Boyd, *op. cit.*, p. 42.

5. *Ibid.*

6. Layton P. Zimmer, "The People of the Underground Church," in Boyd, *op. cit.*, pp. 7 ff.

7. *Ibid.*, pp. 12 ff.

8. H. R. Niebuhr, *Christ and Culture* (Harper & Brothers, 1951), pp. 83–116.

9. Boyd, *op. cit.*, p. 240.

10. Peter Berger, "The Relevance Bit Comes to Canada," in *The Restless Pew*, ed. by William Kilbourn (J. B. Lippincott Company, 1966), p. 75.

11. *Ibid.*, p. 77.

12. Zimmer, in Boyd, *op. cit.*, p. 21.

13. *Ibid.*, p. 20; cf. Baum, *op. cit.*, pp. 196–210.

14. Poling, *op. cit.*, p. ix.

15. William A. Holmes, *The Cosmopolitan Community* (Abingdon Press, 1967), p. 55.

16. Michael Novak, "The Revolution of 1976," p. 441.

17. Gordon Cosby, "Not Renewal, But Reformation," in *Who's Killing the Church?* ed. by Stephen Rose.

18. Gordon Cosby, in *Christian Advocate*, Sept. 12, 1963, pp. 7–10.

19. Holmes, *op. cit.*, p. 54.

Chapter 6 TOWARD A CONSERVING RADICALISM

1. Cf. Paul Ramsey, *Who Speaks for the Church?* (Abingdon Press, 1967).

2. Georg Wilhelm Friedrich Hegel, *The Philosophy of History,* tr. by J. Sibree (Dover Publications, Inc., 1956); *Lectures on the Philosophy of Religion,* tr. by E. B. Speirs and J. Burdon Sanderson (Humanities Press, Inc., 1962), "The Realization of Spiritual Community," pp. 123 ff.

3. Karl Marx and Friedrich Engels, *Basic Writings on Politics and Philosophy* (Doubleday & Company, Inc., 1959), pp. 262 ff.; George H. Sabine, *A History of Political Theory* (Henry Holt & Co., Inc., 1955), pp. 620 ff.

4. Georg Wilhelm Friedrich Hegel, *On Christianity: Early Theological Writings* (Harper & Brothers, 1948), pp. 145 ff.

5. If earlier we warned against the messianic pretensions of the revolutionary mentality, we are not now turning to applaud these pretensions as such, but rather simply pointing out that they play a crucial and significant, albeit limited, kairotic role in the process of historic change.

6. Hugh A. Reyburn, *The Ethical Theory of Hegel* (Oxford: Clarendon Press, 1921), p. 14.

7. See Paul Tillich, *The Protestant Era* (The University of Chicago Press, 1957), Ch. III, "Kairos."

8. Peter Viereck (ed.), *Conservatism: From John Adams to Churchill* (D. Van Nostrand Company, Inc., 1956); Peter Viereck, *Conservatism Revisited: The Revolt Against Revolt* (Charles Scribner's Sons, 1949).

9. Wolfhart Pannenberg (ed.), *Offenbarung als Geschichte* (Göttingen: Vandenhoeck & Ruprecht, 1961), pp. 91 ff.

10. Sabine, *op. cit.,* pp. 636 ff.

11. Such an affirmation does not imply that we become uncritically oblivious to certain dangers in Hegel's thoughts. Among them: (1) He idealizes institutional structures. (2) There is a tendency to authoritarianism. He sometimes seems to view the state as absolutely rational, or to identify it with some divine sanction. (3) There is a tendency to identify what is with what ought to be. (4) The idealization of power tends to develop an attitude of contempt for idealism. (5) Power often

seems self-justifying. (6) Although the Anglo-Saxon concept of individual freedom may need a Teutonic and Hegelian corrective, both actually need to be in balance. The English tradition of individual freedom and rights will be neglected only at our peril. (7) There is a tendency to vagueness and nonspecificity in the dialectic. There is an arbitrariness in its application. (8) The notion of conflict as a means of change can become horribly destructive when the revolutionary tends to imagine that any kind of conflict whatsoever will in some way become creative. (9) There is a tendency toward Machiavellian cynicism in Hegel which advises the politically motivated individual simply to get on board the more promising historical forces. This can deteriorate into an "other-directed ethic," in Riesman's terms, an "antenna morality" which looks around at how things are going, jumps that way, and calls it moral. (10) Although Hegel accorded Christianity an honored place in the dialectic of history, Christian theology must beware of uncritically identifying itself too closely with the Hegelian tendency to cultural accommodation, affirmation of the *status quo,* identification of Christianity with the *Zeitgeist* whatever it might be. Despite all these temptations and objections, however, Hegel speaks to current revolutionary social change with amazing relevance precisely at those points where nondialectical, nonhistorical, anti-institutional thinking is most myopic. J. N. Findlay, *Hegel: A Re-examination* (Collier Books, 1962), pp. 332–350; Sabine, *op. cit.,* pp. 636 ff.; Wolf-Dieter Marsch, *Gegenwart Christi in der Gesellschaft: Eine Studie zu Hegels Dialektik* (Munich: Chr. Kaiser Verlag, 1965), pp. 130 ff., 176–203; Reyburn, *The Ethical Theory of Hegel,* Chs. X–XIII.

12. Hegel, *The Philosophy of History, passim;* Georg Wilhelm Friedrich Hegel, *The Phenomenology of Mind,* tr. by J. B. Baillie (London: George Allen & Unwin, Ltd., 1949), 2d ed., pp. 67–130, 456–679; Marsch, *op. cit.,* Ch. 3, "Hegels Dialektik im Gesellschaftlichen Dasein," pp. 130 ff.

13. Hegel, *On Christianity: Early Theological Writings,* pp. 67 ff.; *The Philosophy of History,* pp. 10 ff.; *The Phenomenology of Mind,* pp. 206 f., 509 ff.; *The Logic of Hegel,* tr. by W. Wallace (Oxford, 1873), pp. 221 ff., 147–151.

Chapter 7 THE STRANGE CASE OF THE INVISIBLE CHURCH

1. The Letters of Ignatius, in *Early Christian Fathers,* ed. by Cyril C. Richardson (The Library of Christian Classics, Vol. I) (The Westminster Press, 1953), pp. 74–120; see J. N. D. Kelly, *Early Christian Doctrines* (Harper & Brothers, 1959), p. 190.

2. Rudolf Bultmann, *Primitive Christianity in Its Contemporary Setting* (Meridian Books, Inc., 1956), pp. 162 ff.; Kelly, *op. cit.,* pp. 190–193.

3. A. Roberts and J. Donaldson (eds.), *The Ante-Nicene Fathers,* Vol. I (Wm. B. Eerdmans Publishing Company, 1951), pp. 552 ff.; Kelly, *op. cit.,* pp. 191–192.

4. Matt. 13: 24–30; cf. Kelly, *op. cit.,* pp. 200 f.

5. F. Crombie, tr., *The Writings of Origen* (Edinburgh: T. & T. Clark, 1889), Vol. I, pp. 72 ff., Vol. II, pp. 126–128, 464.

6. Cyprian, *The Unity of the Catholic Church,* tr. by M. Bevenot, S.J. (The Newman Press, 1957); cf. B. C. Butler, *The Idea of the Church* (Helicon Press, Inc., 1962), pp. 88 ff.

7. Reinhold Seeberg, *Textbook of the History of Doctrines,* tr. by C. E. Hay (Baker Book House, 1952), Vol. II, pp. 313–315; cf. Kelly, *op. cit.,* pp. 410–412.

8. Kelly, *op. cit.,* p. 413. See Augustine, "On Baptism," *Writings in Connection with the Donatist Controversy,* tr. by J. R. King, Book I (Edinburgh: T. & T. Clark, 1872).

9. Stanislaus J. Grabowski, *The Church: An Introduction to the Theology of St. Augustine* (Herder & Herder, Inc., 1957), pp. 205 ff.; cf. Kelly, *op. cit.,* p. 415.

10. Augustine, "On Baptism," section 5; quoted by Kelly, *op. cit.,* p. 416.

11. *Augustine: Earlier Writings,* ed. by John H. S. Burleigh (The Library of Christian Classics, Vol. VI) (The Westminster Press, 1953), pp. 231–235; 289–322; *Augustine: Later Works,* tr. by John Burnaby (The Library of Christian Classics, Vol. VIII) (The Westminster Press, 1955), pp. 268–272, 339 ff.

12. Athanasius, *The Incarnation of the Word of God* (The Macmillan Company, 1946).

13. John Oman, "The Church," *Encyclopedia of Religion*

and Ethics, ed. by James Hastings (Charles Scribner's Sons, 1951), Vol. III, p. 622.

14. Ernst Troeltsch, *The Social Teachings of the Christian Churches,* Vol. I (London: George Allen & Unwin, Ltd., 1931), pp. 358 ff.

15. Thomas Aquinas, *Summa Theologica,* 3a. viii. 1, and 3a. viii. 3.

16. Martin Luther, *Works of Martin Luther* (St. Louis edition), Vol. 8, p. 101.

17. *Ibid.,* Vol. 5, pp. 1234 f.

18. *Ibid.,* Vol. 4, pp. 2014 f.

19. *Ibid.,* Vol. 18, p. 1017.

20. Seeberg, *op. cit.,* Vol. II, pp. 354 f.

21. John Calvin, *Institutes of the Christian Religion* (London: James Clarke & Company, Ltd., 1953), Vol. II, pp. 280 ff.; IV. i and ii.

22. Seeberg, *op. cit.,* Vol. II, p. 409; Calvin, *op. cit.,* pp. 283 ff.

23. Calvin, *op. cit.,* IV. iii–v. Cf. A. M. Hunt, *The Teaching of Calvin* (London: James Clarke & Company, Ltd., 1950), pp. 152–214; Wilhelm Niesel, *The Theology of Calvin* (The Westminster Press, 1956); T. F. Torrance, *Kingdom and Church* (Essential Books, Inc., 1956), pp. 125 ff.

24. Heinrich Heppe, *Reformed Dogmatics* (London: George Allen & Unwin, Ltd., 1950), pp. 658–668. Cf. H. R. Niebuhr, *Christ and Culture,* pp. 217 ff., and *The Kingdom of God in America* (Harper & Brothers, 1937).

25. Richard Hooker, *The Laws of Ecclesiastical Polity,* III. i. 14, from *Works,* ed. by J. Keble, Vol. I, pp. 350 ff.

26. H. F. Woodhouse, *The Doctrine of the Church in Anglican Theology 1547–1603* (The Macmillan Company, 1954), pp. 48–50.

27. Robert Bellarmine, *Disputationes de controversiis christianae fidei, De ecclesia militante,* II. Cf. J. Brodrick, S.J., *The Life and Works of Blessed Robert Cardinal Bellarmine* (1928), Vol. II; Geddes MacGregor, *Corpus Christi* (The Westminster Press, 1958), pp. 96 ff.

28. MacGregor, *Corpus Christi,* p. 74.

29. *Ibid.,* p. 237. Cf. Edmund S. Morgan, *Visible Saints: The History of a Puritan Idea* (New York University Press, 1963);

and *The Reformation of the Church,* ed. by Iain Murray (London: Banner of Truth Trust, 1965), for a further discussion of Puritan ecclesiology.

30. Leonard Verduin, *The Reformers and Their Stepchildren* (Wm. B. Eerdmans Publishing Company, 1964).

31. Franklin H. Littell, *The Free Church* (Starr King Press, 1957), pp. 113 ff.

32. Franklin H. Littell, *The Origins of Sectarian Protestantism: A Study of the Anabaptist View of the Church* (The Macmillan Company, 1964), pp. 82 ff.

Chapter 8   THE REVOLUTIONARY NOW

1. Geddes MacGregor, *The Coming Reformation* (The Westminster Press, 1960), pp. 47 ff.; William Stringfellow, *Dissenter in a Great Society* (Holt, Rinehart & Winston, Inc., 1966), "The Orthodoxy of Radical Involvement," pp. 125 ff.

2. Cf. Albert Mirgeler, *Mutations of Western Christianity,* tr. by E. Quinn (Herder & Herder, Inc., 1964), esp. pp. 66 ff., 121 ff., 130 ff.

3. Job 13:15.

4. For the seminal discussion on this, see Philippe Maury, *Politics and Evangelism* (Doubleday & Company, Inc., 1959), Chs. II and III.

5. Charles West, *Outside the Camp* (Doubleday & Company, Inc., 1959), "The Shaking of Our Confidence," pp. 13 ff.

Chapter 9   DYING FORMS OF A LIVING TRADITION

1. Maury, *op. cit.,* pp. 1–51; J. Robert Nelson, *The Christian Student and the Church* (Association Press, 1952), pp. 1–28.

2. Wilmore, *op. cit.,* Ch. I, "The Protestant Trap."

3. Hans Lilje, *Kirche und Welt* (Munich: Paul List, 1956); Gogarten, *op. cit.*

Chapter 10   RADICAL THEOLOGY AND THE INSTITUTIONAL CHURCH

1. Thomas C. Oden, *Radical Obedience: The Ethics of Rudolf Bultmann,* with a response by Rudolf Bultmann (The

Westminster Press, 1964).

2. Dietrich Bonhoeffer, *Ethics* (London: SCM Press, Ltd., 1955), pp. 55, 178–185; *Prisoner for God* (The Macmillan Company, 1957), pp. 145 f.

3. Bonhoeffer, *Ethics,* p. 61.

4. H. R. Niebuhr, *Christ and Culture,* pp. 84, 101 ff.

5. Cf. C. W. Christian and G. R. Wittig, *Radical Theology: Phase Two* (J. B. Lippincott Company, 1967).

6. Schubert M. Ogden, *The Reality of God and Other Essays* (Harper & Row, Publishers, Inc., 1966), pp. 21 ff.

7. George W. Webber, *The Congregation in Mission* (Abingdon Press, 1965), pp. 48–73; *New Directions in Faith and Order,* Bristol, 1967 (Geneva: World Council of Churches, 1968).

8. Thomas Wieser (ed.), *Planning for Mission* (London: The Epworth Press, Publishers, 1966); Oden, "Laity and Vocation: A Review Article," pp. 484 ff.

Chapter 11   THE SOCIAL WELFARE STATE:
A CHANGING CONTEXT FOR A CHANGING MISSION

1. For various historical interpretations, see Franklin H. Littell, *From State Church to Pluralism* (Doubleday & Company, Inc., 1962); H. R. Niebuhr, *The Kingdom of God in America;* C. H. Hopkins, *The Rise of the Social Gospel in America* (Yale University Press, 1940); Timothy Smith, *Revivalism and Social Reform* (Harper & Row, Publishers, Inc., 1965).

2. Rauschenbusch, *Christianity and the Social Crisis,* p. 211; Walter Rauschenbusch, *A Theology of the Social Gospel* (The Macmillan Company, 1917), pp. 38 ff.

3. For penetrating interpretations of the relation of witness and service, see Maury, *op. cit.;* Webber, *The Congregation in Mission,* pp. 70 ff.; Lewis S. Mudge, *In His Service* (The Westminster Press, 1959).